D0633210

TEH OCT 15 '92
BEALE SEP 07 2004

J921 JUAREZ WEP
Wepman, Denis.
Benito Juarez /

DEMCO

BENITO JUÁREZ

Dennis Wepman

1986
CHELSEA HOUSE PUBLISHERS
NEW YORK
NEW HAVEN   PHILADELPHIA

SENIOR EDITOR: William P. Hansen
PROJECT EDITOR: Marian W. Taylor
CAPTIONS: John Haney
EDITORIAL COORDINATOR: Karyn Gullen Browne
EDITORIAL STAFF: Maria Behan
          Emily Bestler
          Perry Scott King
          Kathleen McDermott
          Alma Rodriguez-Sokol
LAYOUT: Irene Friedman
ART ASSISTANTS: Noreen Lamb
          Carol McDougall
          Victoria Tomaselli
COVER ILLUSTRATION: Michael Garland
PICTURE RESEARCH: Brian Araujo

Copyright © 1986 by Chelsea House Publishers, a division of
Chelsea House Educational Communications, Inc. All rights reserved.
Printed and bound in the United States of America.

Frontispiece courtesy of Bettmann Archive

First Printing

Library of Congress Cataloging in Publication Data

Wepman, Dennis. BENITO JUÁREZ.

    (World leaders past & present)
    Bibliography: p.
    Includes index.
    1. Juárez, Benito, 1806–1872. 2. Mexico—Presidents—
Biography.   I. Title.   II. Series.
F1233.J9W47   1986   972'.07'0924 [B] [92] 86-6802
ISBN 0-87754-537-5

Chelsea House Publishers

133 Christopher Street, New York, NY 10014

345 Whitney Avenue, New Haven, CT 06510

5014 West Chester Pike, Edgemont, PA 19028

Contents

CHELSEA HOUSE PUBLISHERS

WORLD LEADERS PAST & PRESENT

ADENAUER
ALEXANDER THE GREAT
MARC ANTONY
KING ARTHUR
ATATÜRK
ATTLEE
BEGIN
BEN-GURION
BISMARCK
LÉON BLUM
BOLÍVAR
CESARE BORGIA
BRANDT
BREZHNEV
CAESAR
CALVIN
CASTRO
CATHERINE THE GREAT
CHARLEMAGNE
CHIANG KAI-SHEK
CHURCHILL
CLEMENCEAU
CLEOPATRA
CORTÉS
CROMWELL
DANTON
DE GAULLE
DE VALERA
DISRAELI
EISENHOWER
ELEANOR OF AQUITAINE
QUEEN ELIZABETH I
FERDINAND AND ISABELLA
FRANCO

FREDERICK THE GREAT
INDIRA GANDHI
MOHANDAS GANDHI
GARIBALDI
GENGHIS KHAN
GLADSTONE
GORBACHEV
HAMMARSKJÖLD
HENRY VIII
HENRY OF NAVARRE
HINDENBURG
HITLER
HO CHI MINH
HUSSEIN
IVAN THE TERRIBLE
ANDREW JACKSON
JEFFERSON
JOAN OF ARC
POPE JOHN XXIII
LYNDON JOHNSON
JUÁREZ
JOHN F. KENNEDY
KENYATTA
KHOMEINI
KHRUSHCHEV
MARTIN LUTHER KING, JR.
KISSINGER
LENIN
LINCOLN
LLOYD GEORGE
LOUIS XIV
LUTHER
JUDAS MACCABEUS
MAO ZEDONG

MARY, QUEEN OF SCOTS
GOLDA MEIR
METTERNICH
MUSSOLINI
NAPOLEON
NASSER
NEHRU
NERO
NICHOLAS II
NIXON
NKRUMAH
PERICLES
PERÓN
QADDAFI
ROBESPIERRE
ELEANOR ROOSEVELT
FRANKLIN D. ROOSEVELT
THEODORE ROOSEVELT
SADAT
STALIN
SUN YAT-SEN
TAMERLANE
THATCHER
TITO
TROTSKY
TRUDEAU
TRUMAN
VICTORIA
WASHINGTON
WEIZMANN
WOODROW WILSON
XERXES
ZHOU ENLAI

ON LEADERSHIP
Arthur M. Schlesinger, jr.

LEADERSHIP, it may be said, is really what makes the world go round. Love no doubt smooths the passage; but love is a private transaction between consenting adults. Leadership is a public transaction with history. The idea of leadership affirms the capacity of individuals to move, inspire, and mobilize masses of people so that they act together in pursuit of an end. Sometimes leadership serves good purposes, sometimes bad; but whether the end is benign or evil, great leaders are those men and women who leave their personal stamp on history.

Now, the very concept of leadership implies the proposition that individuals can make a difference. This proposition has never been universally accepted. From classical times to the present day, eminent thinkers have regarded individuals as no more than the agents and pawns of larger forces, whether the gods and goddesses of the ancient world or, in the modern era, race, class, nation, the dialectic, the will of the people, the spirit of the times, history itself. Against such forces, the individual dwindles into insignificance.

So contends the thesis of historical determinism. Tolstoy's great novel *War and Peace* offers a famous statement of the case. Why, Tolstoy asked, did millions of men in the Napoleonic wars, denying their human feelings and their common sense, move back and forth across Europe slaughtering their fellows? "The war," Tolstoy answered, "was bound to happen simply because it was bound to happen." All prior history predetermined it. As for leaders, they, Tolstoy said, "are but the labels that serve to give a name to an end and, like labels, they have the least possible connection with the event." The greater the leader, "the more conspicuous the inevitability and the predestination of every act he commits." The leader, said Tolstoy, is "the slave of history."

Determinism takes many forms. Marxism is the determinism of class. Nazism the determinism of race. But the idea of men and women as the slaves of history runs athwart the deepest human instincts. Rigid determinism abolishes the idea of human freedom—

the assumption of free choice that underlies every move we make, every word we speak, every thought we think. It abolishes the idea of human responsibility, since it is manifestly unfair to reward or punish people for actions that are by definition beyond their control. No one can live consistently by any deterministic creed. The Marxist states prove this themselves by their extreme susceptibility to the cult of leadership.

More than that, history refutes the idea that individuals make no difference. In December 1931 a British politician crossing Park Avenue in New York City between 76th and 77th Streets around 10:30 P.M. looked in the wrong direction and was knocked down by an automobile—a moment, he later recalled, of a man aghast, a world aglare: "I do not understand why I was not broken like an eggshell or squashed like a gooseberry." Fourteen months later an American politician, sitting in an open car in Miami, Florida, was fired on by an assassin; the man beside him was hit. Those who believe that individuals make no difference to history might well ponder whether the next two decades would have been the same had Mario Constasino's car killed Winston Churchill in 1931 and Giuseppe Zangara's bullet killed Franklin Roosevelt in 1933. Suppose, in addition, that Adolf Hitler had been killed in the street fighting during the Munich *Putsch* of 1923 and that Lenin had died of typhus during World War I. What would the 20th century be like now?

For better or for worse, individuals do make a difference. "The notion that a people can run itself and its affairs anonymously," wrote the philosopher William James, "is now well known to be the silliest of absurdities. Mankind does nothing save through initiatives on the part of inventors, great or small, and imitation by the rest of us—these are the sole factors in human progress. Individuals of genius show the way, and set the patterns, which common people then adopt and follow."

Leadership, James suggests, means leadership in thought as well as in action. In the long run, leaders in thought may well make the greater difference to the world. But, as Woodrow Wilson once said, "Those only are leaders of men, in the general eye, who lead in action. . . . It is at their hands that new thought gets its translation into the crude language of deeds." Leaders in thought often invent in solitude and obscurity, leaving to later generations the tasks of imitation. Leaders in action—the leaders portrayed in this series—have to be effective in their own time.

And they cannot be effective by themselves. They must act in response to the rhythms of their age. Their genius must be adapted, in a phrase of William James's, "to the receptivities of the moment." Leaders are useless without followers. "There goes the mob," said the French politician hearing a clamor in the streets. "I am their leader. I must follow them." Great leaders turn the inchoate emotions of the mob to purposes of their own. They seize on the opportunities of their time, the hopes, fears, frustrations, crises, potentialities. They succeed when events have prepared the way for them, when the community is awaiting to be aroused, when they can provide the clarifying and organizing ideas. Leadership ignites the circuit between the individual and the mass and thereby alters history.

It may alter history for better or for worse. Leaders have been responsible for the most extravagant follies and most monstrous crimes that have beset suffering humanity. They have also been vital in such gains as humanity has made in individual freedom, religious and racial tolerance, social justice and respect for human rights.

There is no sure way to tell in advance who is going to lead for good and who for evil. But a glance at the gallery of men and women in *World Leaders—Past and Present* suggests some useful tests.

One test is this: do leaders lead by force or by persuasion? By command or by consent? Through most of history leadership was exercised by the divine right of authority. The duty of followers was to defer and to obey. "Theirs not to reason why,/ Theirs but to do and die." On occasion, as with the so-called "enlightened despots" of the 18th century in Europe, absolutist leadership was animated by humane purposes. More often, absolutism nourished the passion for domination, land, gold and conquest and resulted in tyranny.

The great revolution of modern times has been the revolution of equality. The idea that all people should be equal in their legal condition has undermined the old structure of authority, hierarchy and deference. The revolution of equality has had two contrary effects on the nature of leadership. For equality, as Alexis de Tocqueville pointed out in his great study *Democracy in America*, might mean equality in servitude as well as equality in freedom.

"I know of only two methods of establishing equality in the political world," Tocqueville wrote. "Rights must be given to every citizen, or none at all to anyone . . . save one, who is the master of all." There was no middle ground "between the sovereignty of all and the absolute power of one man." In his astonishing prediction of 20th-century totalitarian dictatorship, Tocqueville explained how the revolution of equality could lead to the *"Führerprinzip"* and more terrible absolutism than the world had ever known.

But when rights are given to every citizen and the sovereignty of all is established, the problem of leadership takes a new form, becomes more exacting than ever before. It is easy to issue commands and enforce them by the rope and the stake, the concentration camp and the *gulag*. It is much harder to use argument and achievement to overcome opposition and win consent. The Founding Fathers of the United States understood the difficulty. They believed that history had given them the opportunity to decide, as Alexander Hamilton wrote in the first Federalist Paper, whether men are indeed capable of basing government on "reflection and choice, or whether they are forever destined to depend . . . on accident and force."

Government by reflection and choice called for a new style of leadership and a new quality of followership. It required leaders to be responsive to popular concerns, and it required followers to be active and informed participants in the process. Democracy does not eliminate emotion from politics; sometimes it fosters demagoguery; but it is confident that, as the greatest of democratic leaders put it, you cannot fool all of the people all of the time. It measures leadership by results and retires those who overreach or falter or fail.

It is true that in the long run despots are measured by results too. But they can postpone the day of judgment, sometimes indefinitely, and in the meantime they can do infinite harm. It is also true that democracy is no guarantee of virtue and intelligence in government, for the voice of the people is not necessarily the voice of God. But democracy, by assuring the right of opposition, offers built-in resistance to the evils inherent in absolutism. As the theologian Reinhold Niebuhr summed it up, "Man's capacity for justice makes democracy possible, but man's inclination to injustice makes democracy necessary."

A second test for leadership is the end for which power is sought. When leaders have as their goal the supremacy of a master race or the promotion of totalitarian revolution or the acquisition and exploitation of colonies or the protection of greed and privilege or the preservation of personal power, it is likely that their leadership will do little to advance the cause of humanity. When their goal is the abolition of slavery, the liberation of women, the enlargement of opportunity for the poor and powerless, the extension of equal rights to racial minorities, the defense of the freedoms of expression and opposition, it is likely that their leadership will increase the sum of human liberty and welfare.

Leaders have done great harm to the world. They have also conferred great benefits. You will find both sorts in this series. Even "good" leaders must be regarded with a certain wariness. Leaders are not demigods; they put on their trousers one leg after another just like ordinary mortals. No leader is infallible, and every leader needs to be reminded of this at regular intervals. Irreverence irritates leaders but is their salvation. Unquestioning submission corrupts leaders and demands followers. Making a cult of a leader is always a mistake. Fortunately hero worship generates its own antidote. "Every hero," said Emerson, "becomes a bore at last."

The signal benefit the great leaders confer is to embolden the rest of us to live according to our own best selves, to be active, insistent, and resolute in affirming our own sense of things. For great leaders attest to the reality of human freedom against the supposed inevitabilities of history. And they attest to the wisdom and power that may lie within the most unlikely of us, which is why Abraham Lincoln remains the supreme example of great leadership. A great leader, said Emerson, exhibits new possibilities to all humanity. "We feed on genius. . . . Great men exist that there may be greater men."

Great leaders, in short, justify themselves by emancipating and empowering their followers. So humanity struggles to master its destiny, remembering with Alexis de Tocqueville: "It is true that around every man a fatal circle is traced beyond which he cannot pass; but within the wide verge of that circle he is powerful and free; as it is with man, so with communities."

—*New York*

1

The Runaway

The desire to know and to enlighten himself is innate in the heart of man. Free him from the shackles that misery and despotism impose upon him and he will enlighten himself naturally, even if he is not given direct assistance.
—BENITO JUÁREZ

During the early 19th century the Roman Catholic church wielded enormous power in Mexico. It controlled most of the country's schools, owned huge amounts of property, and had an income estimated to be five times greater than the government's. The Church was actually a state within a state and as such, possessed special rights. As a result, the Church and all people connected with it enjoyed a privileged legal status. A priest who committed a crime was always tried by church officials rather than civil authorities.

Early in 1835, the Mexican state of Oaxaca had a Liberal government. Liberals felt that the Church should have fewer special rights and the lower classes more. The citizens of Oaxaca were allowed to petition the courts with legitimate complaints; even the poorest peasant could demand justice. Their chances of receiving it, however, were far greater in the civil courts than in those run by the Church.

One day, a group of Indians in the little town of Loxicha, about 70 miles south of the state's capital (also called Oaxaca), decided to bring a complaint against their village priest. Their case, of course,

THE NEW YORK PUBLIC LIBRARY

Miguel Hidalgo y Costilla, a radical priest in the Mexican village of Dolores, urges his Indian peasant parishioners to overthrow the Spanish colonial government in 1810. Hidalgo was executed by the Spanish authorities the following year, but the revolution he had inspired continued, finally achieving its objective in 1821.

Visiting his home state of Oaxaca, Mexican leader Benito Juárez (1806–72) talks with fellow Zapotec Indians about their problems. Juárez never forgot his humble beginnings; as governor of Oaxaca and later, as president of Mexico, he introduced many reform laws aimed at improving the lot of the poor and powerless.

would have to be heard in an ecclesiastical (church) court. These men could neither read nor write, and the necessary legal procedures were too complicated for them. Fortunately, the villagers knew of a certain lawyer in the state capital who could assist them. Young Benito Juárez, a Zapotec Indian like themselves, had already made something of a name for himself. At 28, he was a deputy member of the state legislature and a part-time teacher of church law at the Institute of Sciences and Arts in Oaxaca — high positions for an Indian at that time. More important, Juárez had a reputation for being sympathetic to the poor and for helping them at no charge if he believed their rights had been violated.

The Indians nervously made their way to the capital. When they reached Juárez's tiny law office, he put them at ease immediately. Barely five feet tall and as dark as they, he did not frighten them with

Mexican Indian laborers cringe under the lash of their Spanish overseer in a 16th-century silver mine. Spain's unrelenting exploitation of Mexico's native population created a deep-seated rage; during the opening stages of the Mexican War of Independence, thousands of Spaniards were massacred by Hidalgo's ragged armies.

ILCE/CONSULATE GENERAL OF MEXICO IN NEW YORK

a show of authority or confuse them with legal jargon, but instead listened attentively to their story. Their village priest, they said, was taking their money and forcing them to work for him without paying the official salary rates. Juárez heard them out, examined their documents carefully, and took the case.

The young lawyer had no illusions about an Indian's chances for justice in the ecclesiastical courts of Mexico, but he was determined to fight for his clients. "Doubtless because of my status as a deputy, and because at that time the state was governed by a Liberal administration," he wrote later, "my appeal was noticed." In fact, the ecclesiastical court not only noticed the appeal, it heeded the argument of the Indians and ordered the priest to make an appearance. He was then suspended from all church duties and told not to return to his parish until his trial.

At that time, however, governments came and went rapidly in Mexico, and the Liberal administration of Oaxaca fell before the trial came up. Once the Conservatives were in power, the ecclesiastical judge reversed his order and told the priest he could return to Loxicha. As soon as he got back, the priest jailed the Indians who had brought the case against him. He then requested — and received — a ruling from the civil authorities ordering imprisonment for any villager who consulted Juárez or any other lawyer about church-related matters.

Juárez was like a bulldog — once he had his teeth in a case, he would not let go. As soon as he learned of his clients' arrest, he set out for Loxicha. There, he demanded to know the charges against his clients and asked to see the warrants for their arrest. The judge flatly refused. When Juárez persisted with his demands, the judge threatened to bring a charge of vagrancy against him.

Outraged, Juárez returned to the capital to make a complaint in the state court. But he was too late. The priest, taking no chances, had already obtained an arrest warrant charging Juárez with "inciting the citizens against the authorities." At midnight the lawyer was seized in his house and taken to a

> *These blows that I suffered, and that daily I saw suffered by the unprotected, confirmed me in my determination to destroy the evil power of the privileged classes.*
> —BENITO JUÁREZ
> on the Loxicha case

jail 60 miles away in Miahuatlán. It took him nine days to get out on bail, and his complaint against the judge was never even answered. To this day, the fate of Juárez's clients remains unknown.

Benito Juárez never forgot the insulting Loxicha incident; both the Catholic church and the state would pay dearly for it. In *Notes for My Children*, written 23 years later, Juárez recounted the episode in detail. "The arbitrary acts of the privileged classes in close association with the civil authority" convinced him, he said, that "society would never be happy while those classes existed in close alliance with public powers." Imprisonment fostered in the young lawyer a desire for justice that would eventually sweep through the entire nation. As Charles Allen Smart writes in his book *Viva Juárez!*: "In the endless hours of those nine days and nights there was forged the will that rocked the Church from its gold foundations, destroyed one empire, and helped bring down another."

Benito Juárez was born in San Paulo Guelatao, in the Mexican state of Oaxaca, on March 21, 1806. Both his parents, "Indians of the primitive race of the country," as he described them, died three years after his birth. Young Benito was left in the inexperienced hands of an unmarried uncle, who lived in the same village.

Oaxaca, in eastern Mexico, is roughly the size of the U.S. state of Indiana. The region's mountains and fertile valleys abound with exotic flowers and animals. Its capital city, Oaxaca, was (and still is) noted for its elaborate churches and monasteries, fine houses, and beautiful public gardens. The people of Oaxaca had long had a reputation for independence and stubborn commitment to preserving their own way of life.

Benito's village consisted of 20 Zapotec Indian families. As in most Indian settlements of the time, there were no schools. Most Zapotecs spoke only their own language; those who also spoke Spanish were rare. For 12 years, young Benito, like most of the village's residents, lived one step above the sheep and goats he tended, and had little more hope of

Since I was dissatisfied with this deplorable method of teaching [at the parish school], I decided to leave the school for good, and to practice by myself.

—BENITO JUÁREZ

self-improvement.

The Zapotecs were familiar with oppression. Between the 4th and the 9th centuries, they had been one of the most powerful and highly advanced tribes in Mexico. They were invaded and conquered first by the Mixtecs and then, in the 12th century, by the Aztecs, a strong and warlike people who sacrificed human prisoners to their war god. In the 1520s the Aztecs were supplanted by Mexico's Spanish conquerors, who continued the tradition of discrimination against the Zapotecs for three more centuries.

As Benito grew up, he realized he would have to leave his village if he were to do more with his life than shepherd animals. The few families who could afford to do so sent their children to the capital for a formal education. Poor families sent their children to work in private homes in the city, on the condition that they would be taught to read and write.

Trying to protect his Mexican Indian flock from enslavement, a 16th-century Catholic missionary extends a crucifix toward a band of heavily armed Spanish adventurers. Liberal priests who were concerned for the welfare of the native population often stood alone against civilian, military, and Church authorities.

THE NEW YORK PUBLIC LIBRARY

Benito had not been so lucky. Although his Uncle Bernardino, a tough, hard-working peasant farmer, often promised to take him to the capital, he never kept his word. Still, he did have some ambition for his nephew. Most professions were closed to the poor — especially to poor Indians — but there was a chance for a career in the Church. With this in mind, Bernardino set his hopes on Benito's becoming a priest. If Benito was accepted as a candidate for the priesthood, he would receive a rigorous education and eventually the prestige and authority that came with association with the Catholic church. It was an ambitious goal, higher than anything ever attempted by a member of his family. It would mean learning to speak, read, and write both Spanish and Latin.

Bernardino himself spoke no Spanish, but he could read a little in his own language, and he taught Benito what he knew. The boy responded eagerly, but the hard life of a Mexican farmer left little time for study. The instruction his uncle could give him in odd moments was painfully limited, and

Spanish landowners in 18th-century Mexico berate their Indian tenant farmers. Throughout the colonial period, and even during the decades following the War for Independence, virtually all the land in Mexico was owned by a handful of private individuals or by the Roman Catholic church.

ILCE/CONSULATE GENERAL OF MEXICO IN NEW YORK

THE NEW YORK PUBLIC LIBRARY

This 19th-century engraving of a "typical" Mexican Indian village romanticizes a way of life that was in reality brutal and harsh. Indian peasants worked very long hours for little reward, and, since most of their villages lacked schools, were largely uneducated.

Benito realized that he was making almost no progress.

On December 17, 1818, the 12-year-old shepherd ran away from home. The flight was a turning point in his life; 40 years later he still remembered the exact date. Juárez himself recounted it very simply. In his *Notes*, he wrote, "I acquired the conviction that I could learn only by going to the city. . . . I was hesitant to leave the house that had sheltered me . . . and to abandon my little friends. . . . The conflict that arose within me, between my feelings and my desire to go to another society . . . where I might acquire an education, was cruel indeed. However, my hunger overcame my emotions. . . ."

This hunger for education was the key passion of Benito Juárez's youth and the driving force that finally pulled him away from his childhood home and friends. Shivering in the cold mountain air, his feet protected only by thin straw sandals, he covered the 41 miles of rugged, rocky country that lay between his home and the capital in one day.

When he entered the city, Benito was penniless. He spoke neither Spanish nor Mixtec, the language

THE NEW YORK PUBLIC LIBRARY

Looking much as they did in Juárez's time, Zapotec women spin thread in Oaxaca in 1908. In 1818 the 12-year-old Juárez, determined to overcome the tradition that kept most Indians illiterate, abandoned his home village for the city of Oaxaca, where he hoped to enroll in school.

used by most of Oaxaca's Indians. All he could do was repeat the name of his sister, who lived in the city. Recognizing her name, a kind stranger finally led the hungry little boy to the home of Antonio Maza, where Benito's sister worked as a cook. The Mazas were a big, friendly family whose house always had room for one more person.

The Mazas, who had come to Mexico from Italy, had done well in their new country. Antonio Maza was a dealer in cochineal, a red dye made from the crushed bodies of a local insect and used to color fabrics. As a foreigner, Maza could never join the upper classes, but he was prosperous. He and his family made their cook's ragged little brother welcome in their home and remained his good friend for the rest of their lives. In time, Benito would become a member of the Maza family by marriage.

He spent three weeks with the Mazas, helping to make the cochineal in return for his keep while he looked for a full-time position as a servant. At last a friend of the Maza family, a bookbinder named

Antonio Salanueva, decided to hire him. This "pious and very honorable man," as Juárez later described him, belonged to the Third Order of St. Francis, whose members, although not actually monks, were closely associated with the Franciscan order and often wore its robes. Before long, Salanueva had enrolled his young servant in a parish school.

Juárez's experiences at his first school were harshly instructive, and gave him his first real insight into the brutal realities of Mexican society. Though the school was small and poor, it was sharply divided by social class. Children who were Spanish or *Creole* — born in Mexico but of Spanish descent — were treated with respect and carefully taught. Indian students were kept apart and given little attention. Although most of the state's population was Indian, native Mexicans were considered scarcely worth teaching. "After some time in the fourth class," Juárez remembered later, "I could still hardly write at all."

The injustice of the situation offended young Benito, as injustice was to offend him all his life. He

Juárez described his birthplace, the village of San Paulo Guelatao, as "mud-walled, flat-roofed, set in pleasant orchards and little fields." He later wrote that the conflict between his affection for the village and his desire to leave it in order to get an education was "cruel indeed."

NATIONAL GEOGRAPHIC

Any people can be free that wants to be.
—FATHER HIDALGO Y COSTILLA
Mexican priest and
revolutionary, 1810

Mexicans of various social classes relax in a park near Guanajuato in the mid-19th century. Juárez gained his first real insight into Mexican society's rigid class divisions at his first school, where children who were Spanish or of Spanish descent were much more carefully educated than their Indian classmates.

soon left the parish school and, since there was no other school open to him, worked on his own, trying to spell out the still unfamiliar Spanish words in Salanueva's books. His employer, a very religious man, was also open-minded and liberal. He owned a large and varied library, and the real beginnings of Juárez's intellectual development took place under his sympathetic influence.

The boy soon realized that, however well-intentioned his benefactor's guidance, he would profit more from a formal education in a real school. He began to think seriously of studying for the priesthood, as his uncle had originally suggested.

Holy Cross Seminary was the largest and best school in the area. As the Church did not discriminate between rich and poor, everyone was equal there, and all were taken seriously. It was the general opinion, he remembered many years later, that

BRADLEY SMITH

THE NEW YORK PUBLIC LIBRARY

María Josefa Juárez introduces her brother Benito to Antonio Salanueva, a Oaxaca bookbinder. Salanueva, who was to employ Benito as a servant from 1819 to 1821, was a devout Catholic whose liberal views on politics and education profoundly influenced the young man.

"priests, and even those studying to become priests, knew a great deal . . . and they were treated with respect and consideration for the knowledge that was attributed to them." Though he never really wanted to be a priest, at 15 he fiercely desired that knowledge — and the respect that went with it. Salanueva was pleased that the boy wanted to enter the seminary. Because the Church needed native-speaking priests, Juárez could study without paying tuition.

The world in which Benito grew to manhood was changing at a rapid pace. As the young Indian prepared to leave his childhood behind and enter Holy Cross Seminary, Mexico's long War for Independence against its Spanish rulers drew to a close. After 11 bloody years of guerrilla warfare, Mexico was now on its own.

The cathedral in Dolores, Mexico, where Miguel Hidalgo y Costilla delivered the sermon that sparked the Mexican War for Independence in 1810. "My children," he cried, "will you be free? Will you make the effort to recover from the hated Spaniards the lands stolen from your forefathers 300 years ago?"

The Mexican War for Independence had begun on the night of September 15, 1810, when a parish priest named Miguel Hidalgo y Costilla cried out for liberty from his pulpit in the town of Dolores. Within a year, the Indians, *mestizos* (offspring of European and Indian parents), and Creoles who had rallied to Hidalgo's cry were overwhelmed by Spanish troops, and Father Hidalgo's neatly severed head was publicly displayed in an iron cage as a warning to others.

THE NEW YORK PUBLIC LIBRARY

THE NEW YORK PUBLIC LIBRARY

The well-disciplined Spanish troops had stopped the mouth that uttered the famous *grito* ("cry") *de Dolores*, but the sound would not be stilled. By the time the dried head of the parish priest was reverently taken down from the granary where it had hung for a decade, Mexico had thrown off the Spanish yoke.

Although the war brought to an end three centuries of Spanish rule, it did not immediately result in Mexican independence. For that, the country still had to wait. Mexico was too accustomed to rule by force to take proper advantage of its new liberty. The nation was still handicapped by a privileged clergy, power-hungry military officers, and a system of vast private estates that took land from Indian villages.

No one could know it then — least of all the earnest young Indian struggling with his Latin grammar — but it was for Benito Juárez that the country was waiting.

Mexican peasants attack a government building during the Mexican War for Independence. Although Spanish rule in Mexico ended in 1821, the country's basic social and political structure remained largely unchanged: the clergy, the military, and the landowners were still very much in control.

2

The Young Lawyer

And this one whom you see here, so serious and reserved, this one will be a great politician. [Juárez] will rise higher than any of us, and he will be one of our great men and the glory of our country.
—MIGUEL MENDEZ
professor at the Oaxaca Institute of Sciences and Arts, 1828

The life of 15-year-old seminarian Benito Juárez was almost untouched by the political storms raging in Mexico. He was still too busy establishing his own independence and equality to be much troubled by the nation's difficulties. He worked hard, got good grades, and learned to read and write Latin. From 1821 to 1827 he also studied religious philosophy, church law, and theology.

By 1827 Juárez had finished all the courses the seminary offered. He wanted to learn more, but there were no advanced schools in Oaxaca. The only way to study science, art, law, or business was to travel to the national capital or to go to another country. Both options were too expensive for Juárez, and he had no real calling to the priesthood, for which his training had prepared him. Fortunately for the young scholar, the liberal state government in Oaxaca chose this time to set up a civil college called the Institute of Sciences and Arts. Eager to attend, Juárez asked Salanueva, whose feelings were very important to him, if he could enroll in the new school. Although the devout old man had hoped his friend would join the priesthood, he gave his blessing to Benito's secular ambitions. In 1828

In 1828 Juárez enrolled at Oaxaca's Institute of Sciences and Arts, a civil college established by the Liberal state government. The secular, or non-religious, school was a radical departure for the region's educational system, which had previously been strictly controlled by the Catholic church.

ILCE/CONSULATE GENERAL OF MEXICO IN NEW YORK

Originally a Spanish loyalist during the Mexican War for Independence, José Antonio López de Santa Anna de Lebrun joined the rebels when he realized their victory was inevitable. Charismatic and ruthlessly self-serving, Santa Anna personified the authoritarian conservatism that Juárez detested.

THE NEW YORK PUBLIC LIBRARY PICTURE COLLECTION

the 22-year-old Juárez entered the institute.

Here at last was the school he had dreamed of — a truly open-minded "community of scholars" that encouraged independent thinking and taught a wide range of subjects. Not surprisingly, the Catholic church was alarmed by the institute. Under the protection of Spain's Catholic kings, Mexico's clergy had monopolized education for three centuries. Newly powerful liberal politicians, with their free-thinking approach to education, were now threatening an established Catholic right. "Under the very powerful influence they exercised at that time on civil authority," Juárez wrote, the clergy "declared a systematic and cruel war" on the new school, which it called "a house of prostitution."

Juárez supported liberal education because he believed it possible to feel sincere religious faith while at the same time wishing to limit the overextended powers of the Church in his country. Others, including some members of the clergy, agreed with

ORGANIZATION OF AMERICAN STATES

him. Juárez was to fight the power of Mexico's religious establishment all his adult life, but he never ceased to consider himself a good Catholic or to draw inspiration from the many enlightened priests of the Church. In fact, no small number of its most devout members were his ardent supporters.

The young man approached his broadened course of studies with great enthusiasm. He began by studying physics, and by 1830 had mastered the subject so thoroughly that he was appointed to teach it as a substitute professor. He quickly realized, however, that his real vocation was the law, which he made his major field of study. Juárez's sober devotion to his studies and his high moral standards were noticed by his teachers. Even then, he was recognized as a man with an important destiny.

During his three years at the institute, Juárez supported himself with odd jobs. In December 1829, while working as a waiter, he had his first encounter

Mexico City in the early 19th century. The Mexican capital was then — as it has continued to be — the country's most important center of commerce, industry, and learning.

with a man who would have a great influence on both Mexico and on Juárez himself. It is one of the ironies of Mexican history that Benito Juárez once served food to José Antonio López de Santa Anna de Lebrun.

Santa Anna, as this Creole is more simply known to history, was the Mexican-born son of a rich Spanish family. Nearly six feet tall, he was slender and muscular, with dark hair and large, sensitive eyes. According to one description, "his deceptively languid manner, . . . graceful speech, and courtly manners often threw his detractors completely off guard. His greatest asset was his voice, which was credited with the ability to paralyze men with its thunder of authority and, moments later, cajole them with its velvet softness."

As an officer in the Spanish army in Mexico, Santa Anna had fought against Father Hidalgo's supporters in the War for Independence. When he saw the tide turning against Spain, however, he switched sides, gaining the rank of brigadier general in the revolutionary army at the age of 26. When the war ended, he became a follower of another defector from the Spanish army, Agustín de Iturbide.

Iturbide, a military hero who played a vital role in gaining Mexico's independence from Spain, became a popular idol after the war. As Mexico puzzled over what form of government it should establish, Iturbide took advantage of his reputation and declared himself emperor. It was not long before the postwar chaos of the country, together with Iturbide's own unscrupulous and dictatorial behavior, brought his reign to an end. After nine months, Emperor Agustín I was overthrown and driven out of the country, marking the end of the first Mexican empire. When Iturbide returned to Mexico the next year, in 1824, he was arrested and shot.

The revolt against Iturbide had been led by his former supporter, Santa Anna, who proclaimed the first Mexican republic in 1823. During the next few decades, a succession of presidents came and went. Some, like Iturbide, were greedy, self-serving men who were forced out of office by indignant patriots. Others were honorable and dedicated, but too weak

> *We few students who attended the courses were frowned upon and ostracized by the immense majority, ignorant and fanatical, of that unhappy community.*
> —BENITO JUÁREZ
> on the persecution of the Oaxaca Institute of Sciences and Arts

to control the ambitious politicians and generals around them. The name of one man, however, appears often in the annals of those tempestuous days: that of the clever aristocrat, Santa Anna.

In 1829, a Spanish effort to regain possession of Mexico led to a brief skirmish in Tampico. The Mexican army, aided by the sweltering heat and a yellow-fever epidemic, defeated the Spanish troops, but Santa Anna claimed credit for the victory. As the "hero of Tampico," he was given a celebratory banquet in Oaxaca.

It was at the banquet that Santa Anna first encountered the young Indian who was to be his greatest political enemy for nearly half a century. Years later, when he learned who the waiter had been, Santa Anna said it must have been envy that had turned Juárez against him. "He could not forgive me," Santa Anna wrote, "because he had waited on me at the table with his bare feet. . . . It is amazing that an Indian of such low degree should have become the figure in Mexico that we all know." Like many Creoles, Santa Anna was never able to accept the idea of an Indian in government.

Social issues were probably far from the mind of young Juárez as he served food to Santa Anna. He was working hard to get through school, and he watched the political scene, if at all, from a safe distance. In 1831 he finished his studies and began to work in a law office. That same year, the 25-year-old Juárez took his first cautious step into politics. He ran for city alderman, and won. He was now on his way.

Mexico in the mid-19th century was potentially one of the richest countries in the world. It was endowed with tremendous mineral resources (its mines were already producing one-half of the world's silver) and highly fertile land. Despite its natural wealth, however, Mexico was a backward country and culturally unprepared for self-government. During the 10 years since it had become a republic, one politician after another had seized power and been overthrown. The bulk of the Mexican people, largely illiterate and accustomed to poverty and oppression, saw little difference among

[Santa Anna's] conscience was elastic and numb, never disturbed by actions that would have disturbed most men.
—HUBERT H. BANCROFT
American historian

31

these constantly changing leaders. They accepted the political chaos of their country as a natural phenomenon.

The most important political organizations in Mexico were the Liberal and the Conservative parties. Liberals were in favor of free elections, equal distribution of land, and the abolition of class distinctions and special privileges for the wealthy and the Catholic church. Members of the Liberal party included middle-class intellectuals, journalists, teachers, and lawyers. Conservatives favored a centralized government, and supported the Catholic church, the army, and a ruling, landowning class. The party attracted members of the clergy, army officers, businessmen, peasants, and Indians.

Mexico seesawed between these two parties for years, and one rebellion followed another. In 1829 revolutionary hero Vicente Guerrero headed a Liberal government supported by Santa Anna. In 1830 Guerrero was seized by his Conservative vice-president, Anastasio Bustamante, forced to kneel in public as he heard his death sentence read, and then shot. Bustamante's dictatorial regime lasted less than two years; he was overthrown in 1832 by Santa Anna, who in 1833 took over the presidency himself.

The riots that followed were horrifyingly routine by then. Conservative gangs in Oaxaca tried to regain power for their party, and the 27-year-old Juárez joined the state militia. Appointed aide to the general who was defending Oaxaca against the rioters, he took part in a series of bloody street fights, displaying the physical courage for which he was to become famous. His bravery earned him the rank of captain in the militia.

In the same year — 1833 — Juárez was elected to the Oaxaca state legislature. It was an important post for an Indian and he played his hand very carefully, trying to offend neither the Liberals nor the Conservatives. The only measure he introduced called for the construction of an official memorial for the executed President Guerrero. Modest as it was, this proposal earned him the strong disapproval of the Conservatives.

In 1834 Juárez's professional life took a turn upward when he was formally recognized as an attorney by the state court of justice. Although he had practiced law for three years and had held several public offices since earning his law degree, he had never taken the examination that would give him the official title of advocate and the authority to plead cases before the state's higher courts. When he finally sat for the tests, he did so well that he was named an acting judge of the state court. He held the office only briefly, however; following the fall from power of Oaxaca's Liberal government, all its

Liberal priest José María Morelos y Pavón leads his peasant followers against Spanish troops during the Mexican War for Independence. Juárez greatly admired Morelos, whose many revolutionary victories included the capture of Oaxaca in 1812.

ILCE/CONSULATE GENERAL OF MEXICO IN NEW YORK

officials, including Juárez, were arrested. Juárez was confined in the city of Tehuacán for several days. Nothing further came of it then, but the incident foretold of difficult days ahead.

Juárez had thus far dedicated himself to the law and to the justice it represented, but he had not considered himself a reformer. The injustice suffered by his Indian clients at Loxicha, however, along with his own arrest in Tehuacán, persuaded him that Mexican politics had to be reformed once and for all. Juárez's dream of a successful, respectable life for himself now became a vision of a free and just society for all.

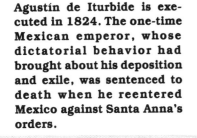

Agustín de Iturbide is executed in 1824. The one-time Mexican emperor, whose dictatorial behavior had brought about his deposition and exile, was sentenced to death when he reentered Mexico against Santa Anna's orders.

THE NEW YORK PUBLIC LIBRARY

Juárez was to keep his indignation to himself for many years. He continued to defend the poor, usually without a fee, and he maintained cordial relationships with the changing governments of his state and nation. Because he remained aloof from politics, Juárez received appointments from both Liberals and Conservatives. In 1841 he became a senior judge in the state capital's court of justice. He was a model judge — learned, patient, and above all, impartial.

Even before he became a judge, Juárez had begun to wear the clothes that would become his trademark: black wool suit, high-collared, white linen shirt, black silk bow tie, and "stovepipe" hat. (It was the same sober uniform as that worn by his American contemporary, Abraham Lincoln.) Throughout his life Juárez was very much of a stoic. He kept himself and his clothing scrupulously clean, slept and ate little, and only occasionally drank wine. A man of reserved habits, he rarely talked about his personal life and, with one or two exceptions, never had or seemed to need a close friend. Guillermo Prieto, once one of his most trusted colleagues, wrote: "In familiar conversation Juárez was very sweet . . . his pleasure was in serving others. . . . I never heard him discredit anyone, and as for modesty, I have never known anyone his superior."

Soon after Juárez's political life began, the United States and Mexico came into conflict for the first of many times. The trouble centered — as it often would — on land. When Mexico gained its independence in 1821, it was the third largest country in the world, after Russia and China. More than three times its present size, it stretched from Panama on the south to the borders of what are now Utah and Colorado on the north. When Iturbide fell in 1823, the Central American territories took advantage of the confusion to secede and declare themselves independent republics. Meanwhile, settlers from the United States began to eye Mexico's northern areas hungrily.

In 1822, a Virginian named Stephen Fuller Austin had founded a large American colony in Coahuila, Mexico, in the northern part of what is now the state

> *[Juárez] considered it the duty of all citizens to serve society when called upon to do so, and to serve it honestly, and at any cost to themselves.*
> —CHARLES ALLEN SMART
> American historian

War hero and leading Liberal Vicente Guerrero became president of Mexico in 1829, but he was ousted by his ultraconservative vice-president, Anastasio Bustamante, the following year. Guerrero, whom Juárez deeply respected, was convicted of treason, forced to kneel in public as his death sentence was read, and then shot.

ILCE/CONSULATE GENERAL OF MEXICO IN NEW YORK

I call on you in the name of liberty, of patriotism, and everything dear to the American character, to come to our aid with all dispatch. If this call is neglected, I am determined to sustain myself as long as possible and die like a soldier who never forgets what is due to his own honor and that of his country. VICTORY OR DEATH.
—WILLIAM BARRET TRAVIS
American commander at
the Alamo, in his
last dispatch, February 1836

of Texas. By 1834 the area contained 20,000 Americans and only some 5,000 Mexicans, and the colonists began to regard the settlement as U.S. territory. Conflict was inevitable.

In becoming Mexican residents, the Americans had renounced their U.S. citizenship, but they continued to speak English and resented any interference in their affairs from Mexican officials. Relations between the Mexican government and its colonists went from bad to worse, and on March 2, 1836, the Texans declared their colony an independent nation.

Santa Anna, then president of Mexico, saw the situation as a perfect opportunity to become a hero once again. Assembling an army of 4,000 men, he marched north to attack the upstart "Republic of Texas." The American colonists banded together to repel the attack. In an abandoned mission building in an aspen grove, 187 Texans under the leadership of American lawyer and soldier William Travis held out for 12 days against Santa Anna's 4,000 soldiers. At last, the Mexicans swept into the mission; Santa Anna had prevailed by sheer weight of numbers. Most of the Texans, who had killed 1,500 soldiers before being defeated, died during the battle. The few who survived were shot on Santa Anna's orders. Among the dead were the celebrated American frontiersmen Jim Bowie and Davy Crockett. The bodies were heaped into a great pile and burned.

The aspen tree — in Spanish, *álamo* — gave a name to the beleaguered fortress, and "Remember the Alamo!" became the Texans' battle cry. Advancing eastward, Santa Anna's army was cut down by General Sam Houston at San Jacinto on April 21, 1836. Santa Anna was captured and, on May 21,

The port of Tampico, where Mexican troops led by Santa Anna repelled an 1829 Spanish invasion. During an Oaxaca banquet celebrating the victory, Santa Anna first encountered the man who would become his lifelong foe: Juárez, who was working his way through school, served a meal to the "Hero of Tampico."

THE NEW YORK PUBLIC LIBRARY

"Let those who choose to stay and die with me step across this line!" American commander William Barret Travis proudly watches his troops respond to these words as they await an attack on the Alamo by Santa Anna's 4,000-man Mexican army on March 6, 1836. All 187 defenders of the Texas mission were killed in the battle that followed.

THE BETTMANN ARCHIVE

THE BETTMANN ARCHIVE

Raising his knife in a last, futile gesture of defiance, Texan Jim Bowie faces Mexican troops at the Alamo in 1836. At Bowie's side is American frontiersman Davy Crockett, another of the 187 Americans who died during Santa Anna's bloody siege of the Texas outpost.

signed a treaty granting independence to Texas.

The Mexican government renounced the concession and unceremoniously removed Santa Anna from office, but it was too late. Texas remained an independent republic until 1845, when it was admitted to the United States as the nation's 28th state.

Juárez was outraged by Santa Anna's behavior, but he kept it to himself and continued to work hard at his job. Soon the distinguished Don Benito was in a position to marry. He had never lost contact with the Mazas, the family who had taken him in when he ran away 25 years earlier, and in 1843 he married Margarita, the Mazas' youngest daughter. He was 37 and she was 17, he a poor Indian and she the daughter of a rich merchant, but it was the best of marriages. The couple would have 12 children, seven of whom they lived to see reach adulthood. Juárez wrote Margarita long, loving letters whenever they were separated, and she became his closest confidante and adviser.

Juárez's "old woman," as he affectionately called her, was to suffer and sacrifice much for her husband, but she always stood firm. Whatever had to be done, she did unhesitatingly. She had known him all her life, and she never doubted his moral stature. "He is very homely," she is reported to have said before their marriage, "but very good."

A judge when he married, Juárez became a justice of the Oaxaca supreme court two years later. The year after that, in 1846, he was elected to represent his state in the country's capital, Mexico City. It was his first step into the arena of national politics. The Indian shepherd boy from the hills had come far, but he still had a long way to go.

Captured Mexican President Santa Anna is brought before General Sam Houston, commander in chief of the Texas provisional government's forces, on April 22, 1836. The day before, Houston's troops had crushed the Mexican army at San Jacinto. One month later, Santa Anna signed away Mexico's claim to Texas.

THE BETTMANN ARCHIVE

3

"I Am a Son of the People"

It is amazing that an Indian of such low degree should have become the figure in Mexico that we all know.
—ANTONIO LÓPEZ DE SANTA ANNA
Mexican general and politician, on Juárez's rise to prominence

Juárez had some idea of how dangerous national politics could be before he ever set foot in the capital. As secretary to the governor of Oaxaca and assistant state attorney, he had witnessed the shifting balance of power as one party succeeded another in office. Despite his attempts at avoiding partisanship, he had spent time in jail for identifying himself too clearly with one side. With the past in mind, the cautious new delegate from Oaxaca found it wiser to wait and watch during his first assignment in the capital. During the bitter debates of the Congress of 1846–47, Juárez sat silent, voting when he had to but volunteering nothing. "In this congress," wrote a Mexican historian, "Juárez was a sphinx."

The debates concerned the Mexican-American War, which had just broken out. Both Mexicans and Americans had expected war. As long as Texas was an independent nation, Mexico could hope someday to retrieve the territory. When it became a part of the United States in 1845, however, Mexico lost Texas permanently, and all Mexican land north of

THE BETTMANN ARCHIVE

James K. Polk, who became the 11th president of the United States in 1845, declared war on Mexico in 1846. Under the terms of the peace treaty that ended the war in 1848, the defeated Mexicans ceded more than 1 million square miles of their territory to their northern neighbor.

General Zachary Taylor (who served as U.S. president from 1849 to 1850) is portrayed as a mass murderer by the famous American lithographer Nathaniel Currier. The 1846–48 Mexican War, in which Taylor led American forces to a series of victories, was popular with some Americans, but regarded as unjust by many others.

THE BETTMANN ARCHIVE

it fell into American hands as well. The United States now claimed that the Rio Grande (the river flowing southeast from the city of El Paso to the Gulf of Mexico) was going to be Mexico's new northern boundary.

The new border meant that Mexico would lose half of its territory. Naturally, the Mexicans resisted. Their anger suited America's purposes very well. If there was any violence, the newly elected U.S. president, James K. Polk, who made no secret of his hunger for Mexican land, could easily get a declaration of war from Congress. He sent General (later president) Zachary Taylor to Mexico with thinly veiled orders to provoke an attack. "Polk baited Mexico into war over the Texas boundary question," according to American historian Samuel Eliot Morison. Taylor went to Mexico in January 1846, and in May one of his scouting parties was ambushed by a Mexican cavalry unit. Congress quickly gave Polk the declaration of war he requested.

The United States called the war a defensive action; Mexico called it an invasion. Both armies, confident of being morally in the right, fought courageously, and both suffered heavy casualties. After two years of resistance, Mexico was forced to surrender Texas with the Rio Grande boundary,

American troops fight off a Mexican cavalry assault in 1847. Juárez, who had been elected to represent Oaxaca in the Mexican national congress in 1846, remained silent during the congressional debates on the Mexican War: "In this congress," observed one historian, "Juárez was a sphinx."

THE LIBRARY OF CONGRESS

plus land now occupied by the states of New Mexico, Colorado, Utah, Nevada, Arizona, and California. The United States paid Mexico the token sum of $15 million for the land. It had been a profitable war for Polk and the United States.

Meanwhile, Juárez, his congressional term over in 1847, had returned to Oaxaca to take up his law practice again and, if necessary, to help defend the province against an American invasion. Back home, the state government was falling apart. The Conservatives were officially in power, but their control of the capital was slipping. When the government of Oaxaca finally fell in late 1847, the state court of justice convened the legislature to name a new governor.

Juárez, by keeping his views private, had made no enemies, and he had acquired a reputation for honesty, justice, and moderation. It was Juárez whom the legislature selected to be acting governor until an election could be held. The next year, in 1848, Juárez was elected governor of the state of Oaxaca by a large majority.

Juárez considered himself a man of the people, and it was the people he served, not the wealthy landowners or the rich, powerful institutions. During his first inauguration, a group of Zapotec Indians from his village arrived bearing gifts of fruit, chicken, and corn. Confident of their old friend's determination to improve their lives, the Indians congratulated him warmly on his election.

The scene moved Juárez deeply; he knew out of what grinding poverty these gifts had come. With a rare display of emotion, he embraced his countrymen and pledged himself always to conduct his life so as to be worthy of their faith. That night, the Indians slept in the hallways of the governor's palace, and the next morning Juárez gave each a gift of money from his own pocket as a token of his pledge.

In 1848, when he was inaugurated for his full term as governor, Juárez made a solemn promise: "I am a son of the people and I shall not forget it. . . . I shall uphold their rights, I shall take care that they become educated, that they lift themselves up, that

This is no war of defense, but one of unnecessary and offensive aggression. It is Mexico that is defending her firesides, her castles and altars, not we.
—HENRY CLAY
American statesman

they make a future for themselves."

He kept his word. In his four years as governor of Oaxaca, he turned that poor state into one of the most prosperous in Mexico. He set up a public health system, tactfully overcoming the Indians' fear and suspicion of vaccinations, and established free clinics and hospitals throughout the state. He started large public projects to stimulate the economy, built roads and bridges to transport crops, and opened a port for foreign trade.

Attaching the highest importance to education, Juárez gave special attention to the schools of Oa-

Laying claim to "the Halls of Montezuma," American General Winfield Scott leads his victorious army into Mexico City on September 14, 1847. Shortly before, Juárez had been named acting governor of Oaxaca. Under his leadership, the state provided both manpower and financing for the continued prosecution of the war.

THE BETTMANN ARCHIVE

xaca. His own beloved Institute of Sciences and Arts received help at once, and he also built over 200 new schools, including eight teachers' colleges. Indians were especially welcome in the public schools. With the revolutionary conviction that the education of women led to a better society, he also encouraged girls to enter the schools. For the first time, everyone in Oaxaca had an equal chance at an education, with no regard to social class or sex.

Perhaps Juárez's most highly acclaimed achievement was his reform of the state's government. Through collecting taxes rigorously and spending the money legally, he greatly reduced Oaxaca's public debt. A careful monetary policy enabled him to pay civil servants adequately and on time, which in turn increased their honesty and efficiency. Dishonest government workers were discharged and competitive examinations instituted for would-be replacements.

Juárez became the first governor in Mexico's history to improve the condition of his state's treasury while in office. He eliminated waste, special privileges, and political favoritism. At the same time, he spent more on regional defenses, construction, and development than any governor ever had.

Juárez never exhibited the showmanship that was so popular in Mexican politics. His actions were not spectacular; his reforms were far-reaching, but unsensational. His success stemmed from a combination of steady, dedicated work and personal courage. Those who knew Juárez said he never tired, never gave up, and never backed down. His courage was both moral and physical. Unlike most of his contemporaries, he rarely carried a weapon. Once, in 1850, when he learned of a mutiny in a military garrison in Oaxaca, he rode over immediately, strode into the barracks unarmed, and calmly ordered the soldiers to resume their duties. His obvious lack of fear and his assured manner had immediate results; order was restored and the mutiny brought to an end without bloodshed.

On at least one occasion, however, his courage would cost him dearly. Early in his administration, Juárez learned that Santa Anna, following his sign-

> *You know what we need, and you will give it to us, because you are good and will not forget that you are one of us.*
> —Indians of Juárez's village, upon his inauguration as governor of Oaxaca

THE LIBRARY OF CONGRESS

Ulysses S. Grant directs artillery fire during the capture
of Mexico City in 1847. Grant, an active military officer
throughout the Mexican War, was named commander of
all U.S. armies during the American Civil War. He served
as president of the United States from 1869 to 1877.

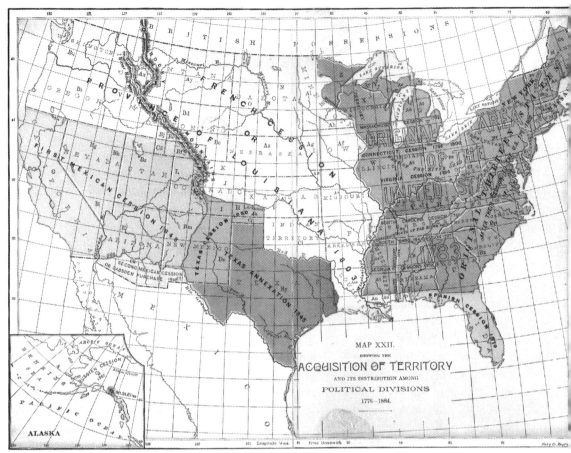

MAP XXII.
SHOWING THE
ACQUISITION OF TERRITORY
AND ITS DISTRIBUTION AMONG
POLITICAL DIVISIONS
1776–1884.

Under the terms of the 1848 U.S.-Mexican peace treaty, Mexico recognized the Rio Grande as its northeastern frontier, renounced its claims to Texas, and ceded to the United States territory now occupied by New Mexico, Colorado, Utah, Nevada, Arizona and California.

ing of the treaty that ceded Texas to the United States, was leading a column of soldiers toward Oaxaca's capital. Juárez was at the moment facing the threat of an uprising by Oaxaca's recently ousted Conservatives. Aware that Santa Anna's presence in the capital could turn the threat into a reality, Juárez issued an order to Santa Anna: the general, he said, would be allowed to go through the state but he was not to approach the capital "because his presence in the city . . . would be harmful to the public order." Santa Anna obeyed the humiliating command. He was in enough trouble for mishandling his command in the war without openly violating a governor's order. Peace was maintained in Oaxaca, but six years later, when Santa Anna returned to power, he remembered the insult and repaid it with interest.

The aristocratic Santa Anna may have loathed the "presumptuous" Juárez, but the public felt otherwise. He had transformed his state into a model of progress and stability, without taking a *centavo* for himself. His reward was the affection of his people and the high esteem of other governors.

Honored and admired, Juárez completed his term as governor of Oaxaca in 1852 and retired to resume his law practice. The Institute of Sciences and Arts invited him to serve as its director, and he eagerly accepted the job at a token salary. He was content to be a private citizen again.

While Juárez had been building a financially sound, stable Oaxaca, the rest of the country had been growing ever more chaotic. The national government had changed hands four times. America's $15 million payment for the Mexican territory it annexed had done little to keep the remainder of the country from bankruptcy. The old conflicts among church, army, and state had resurfaced with new vigor after the war. Indians were rebelling, bandits were terrorizing defenseless towns, Texans were freely raiding border villages, and business had halted almost completely. Mexico was debt-ridden and unable to find a means of salvaging its economy.

Several well-meaning presidents tried to save the country from disintegration, but each time such an official endeavored to cut expenses, the targets of the cut "pronounced" against him and removed him from office. The peculiar Mexican institution called the *pronunciamiento* (declaration) could be a noble cry for liberty — the *grito de Dolores* was, in a sense, a pronunciamiento — but more often it was simply the proclamation of an ambitious general against the government, issued as an excuse for another rebellion. In Mexico, personal relations were traditionally more important than allegiance to a government. Pronunciamientos were so frequent and so successful because most Mexican men followed the ancient practice of placing loyalty to a *patron*, or master, above all else.

Between 1846 and 1852, a long series of pronunciamientos resulted in the removal from office of one president after another. In 1853 an army

The cup of forbearance has been exhausted. After reiterated menaces, Mexico has passed the boundaries of the United States, has invaded our territory, and has shed American blood on American soil.
—JAMES K. POLK
U.S. president (1845–49), asking Congress for a declaration of war against Mexico

Juárez, who was elected to a full term as governor of Oaxaca in 1848, called himself "a son of the people." He promised to "uphold their rights, take care that they become educated, that they lift themselves up, that they make a future for themselves."

THE NEW YORK PUBLIC LIBRARY

mutiny put Lucas Alemán, a wealthy Creole aristocrat, into power. Alemán was an archconservative who had opposed the War for Independence and bitterly resented all reform. He decided that the country needed not a president, but a dictator or a king, who could restore the power of the army and the Catholic church. Accordingly, Alemán persuaded Congress to ask Santa Anna to rule the country until a suitable monarch could be enthroned. Santa Anna, now 60 years old, consented on the condition that he have total, unchallenged control.

Once in power, he established a despotic regime and set up a magnificent court. Unable to resist the trappings of royalty, he assumed the title, "His Most Serene Highness." He soon began bringing his own brand of order to the national capital. He eliminated popular elections, cancelled recent reforms, and returned power to the Catholic church, the army, and the wealthy landowners. One of the dictator's first official acts, as insurance against a possible revolt, was to round up and exile many prominent Liberals. Juárez continued to practice law and run the institute, but he doubted that Santa Anna would leave him in peace for long.

He was correct. A would-be assassin, hired by the Conservative governor Santa Anna had installed in Oaxaca, shot at Juárez in March 1853. The shot missed and the gunman fled, but Juárez was not safe yet. The governor soon removed him as director of the Institute of Sciences and Arts, a move that deeply hurt and angered Juárez. Still, Santa Anna was not finished with his enemy.

In May 1853 Juárez was taking testimony for a case in the town of Etla, near the capital, when he

THE NEW YORK PUBLIC LIBRARY

A mule train negotiates a mountain road in Oaxaca. As governor of the state, Juárez worked hard to improve its economy. He built new roads and bridges to improve transportation, started public-works projects to increase jobs, and developed a seaport to encourage foreign trade.

was unceremoniously arrested by armed soldiers. Given no chance to contact his wife and children, Juárez was hustled off to Jalapa, the capital of the state of Veracruz. There he was held for 75 days on a vague charge of "inciting the people in the region to a class war." He vigorously protested the illegality of his arrest, but his complaints were met with silence. After Jalapa, Juárez was taken to the castle of San Juan de Ulúa, in Veracruz.

The dreadful dungeon of this old fortress is described by Charles Allen Smart in *Viva Juárez!*: "The castle of San Juan de Ulúa . . . is one of the most sinister places of imprisonment imaginable. Some of the windowless cells and galleries, to the heavy walls of which prisoners were sometimes chained standing up, are partly below sea level at high tide, and water drips from the walls of all of them, as in caves. . . . Any of them would suffice to break the health and spirit of any man."

Juárez was held in solitary confinement at San Juan de Ulúa for 12 days. Then he received an order exiling him to Europe. By now, he was too sick to move, but he was put on a departing English ship

The port of New Orleans, Louisiana, in the mid-19th century. Here, in December 1853, Juárez joined other exiled Mexican liberals banished from their country by Santa Anna. It was at this point in his career that Juárez resolved to oppose with force what he called "the evil power of the privileged classes" in Mexico.

THE BETTMANN ARCHIVE

nevertheless. The ship's passengers and crew, moved by the plight of the penniless but uncomplaining ex-governor, took up a collection for him, and the captain allowed him to go ashore in Havana, Cuba, the first port of call. There he stayed, helpless and friendless, for over two months.

Although Juárez had been given no chance to contact his wife after his arrest, she had learned of his fate from others. Margarita, too, had been harassed by Santa Anna's government and had gone into hiding. After learning where her husband was, she appealed to everyone she knew for money and collected $400 to send to him. Her brother, José María Maza, journeyed to Havana to give it to him.

Juárez had been banished to Europe, but the United States held a greater attraction for him. Despite its mistreatment of Mexico, it was the model to which he had always looked for a constitutional society. It was also close to home, and other Liberal exiles had begun to gather there. On December 29, 1853, Juárez and his brother-in-law joined their fellow exiles in New Orleans, Louisiana.

Under Santa Anna's rule, state and local governments were practically nonexistent. The Church's power and wealth had increased dramatically, and the army had grown to include 95,000 men. The press was strictly censored, and all who spoke out against the dictator's regime were jailed or exiled.

Santa Anna was nothing if not shrewd. He had made many mistakes, both on the battlefield and in the president's office, but he had nonetheless usually gained his objectives. His banishment of Benito Juárez, however, had been a serious miscalculation. It transformed a moderate, gentle man into an impassioned reformer. Santa Anna had created his own bitterest foe.

Juárez had been a liberal all his political life. Ever since the incident at Loxicha, he had been opposed to "the evil power of the privileged classes" and had struggled to bring equality and justice to Mexico. He had yearned for reform, but he had never sought change beyond the limits of the courts.

Now he was an outlaw, determined to free his people from Santa Anna at any cost.

THE NEW-YORK HISTORICAL SOCIETY

Juárez's nemesis, Santa Anna, alternated between glory and disgrace during his more than 30 years in Mexican politics. Finally exiled in 1855, he lived abroad for almost two decades. In 1874, he returned to Mexico City, where he died in 1876 — poor, alone, and virtually forgotten.

4

Sparks of Reform

Juárez was an inoffensive liberal known only for his model government of Oaxaca. In his own community he was a man of some consequence, but not until he was deported did he belong to the world.
—RALPH ROEDER
American historian

Now Year's Day, 1854, was not a festive occasion for Benito Juárez. The former supreme court justice and governor of Oaxaca found himself part of a band of destitute Mexican exiles struggling to keep themselves and their dream alive in New Orleans. At that point, the United States was far from hospitable to Mexicans. The two countries had only recently fought a bitter war, and the Americans had not yet forgotten the Alamo. Making life even harder for Juárez, the people of New Orleans classed him as a black man because of his dark skin. He was forced to abide by their discriminatory laws against the black population, which meant, for example, having to be off the streets by nightfall.

The leader of the Mexican community in New Orleans was Melchor Ocampo, a distinguished and wealthy former governor of Michoacán who had been dismissed from office in 1850 by the Conservatives and subsequently exiled by Santa Anna. When Juárez arrived, Ocampo quickly chose him as his closest associate. Together with Ponciano Arriaga, a famous jurist later known as "the father of the constitution," and José María Mata, who was to become Mexico's minister of the treasury, Ocampo

THE BETTMANN ARCHIVE

Juárez found New Orleans, where he lived in exile from December 1854 until June 1855, anything but a paradise. Poverty was widespread, jobs almost nonexistent, and racial prejudice strong. A Zapotec Indian, Juárez was treated by most whites with the contempt they habitually showed "people of color."

A Mexican mural portrays Juárez as the architect of *La Reforma* (the Reform), the Liberal program instituted after Santa Anna's 1855 defeat. The Reform culminated in the Mexican Constitution of 1857, which abolished slavery, gave the vote to all adult males, and assured freedom of speech, the press, assembly, and education.

and Juárez did what they could to agitate for freedom in their country.

The exiles had very little money and found work hard to get. Ocampo's rich estates had been confiscated, but he shared what remained with the others. Juárez's wife had opened a little shop in Etla and she smuggled what she could to her husband. For a time Ocampo was a potter's assistant, and Mata worked as a waiter. Juárez and José Maza rolled cigars, which they sold in saloons. The two brothers-in-law shared an $8-per-month furnished room and fished for their meals in the Mississippi River.

For 18 months Juárez and his friends endured this squalid and frustrating life, talking about revolution but helpless to act. Juárez wrote newspaper articles denouncing Santa Anna and helped Ocampo draft political statements and protests to the Mexican consul, but their efforts received little attention.

Time and hardship were to break the spirits of all but the most loyal and dedicated of the group. Many of the exiles gave up and deserted the cause. One member of the group even returned to Mexico to join Santa Anna. Juárez, by now a passionate revolutionary, was outraged. In a letter to his friend Ocampo, he accused the defector of trading "his existence as a man for that of a contemptible reptile on whom we must all spit!" Such strong language was rare with the mild and dignified Juárez, and shows how close he was to the end of his patience.

Juárez never wavered. His youth had acquainted him with poverty and taught him how to rise above it. He survived a case of yellow fever without medical help, since there was no money for doctors, and he endured abuse and loneliness. Trials that broke the spirits of those around him he bore with fortitude and dignity.

Santa Anna's reign, meanwhile, was growing more troubled every day. After spending public money with reckless abandon, he attempted to raise additional funds by selling off some Mexican land to the Americans, who were still trying to extend their borders. In 1853 General James Gadsden, an American army officer and diplomat representing

To be a complete liberal demands effort, because it requires the spirit to be a complete man.
—MELCHOR OCAMPO
liberal governor of
Michoacán and Juárez ally

U.S. railroad men who wanted to build a line to the Pacific coast, picked up a large strip of present-day Arizona and New Mexico for the United States at the bargain price of $10 million. The Gadsden Purchase enraged the Mexicans, who suddenly remembered that Santa Anna had traded off Texas for his own safety back in 1836, after the scandalous affair of the Alamo. Slowly, murmurs grew to shouts, and complaints became pronunciamientos.

Santa Anna responded with even wilder spending and ever more savage repressions. When his treasury was empty, he borrowed money from Europe, agreeing to whatever interest rates were demanded. He was clearly running out of time. To insure his future, he quietly set up a personal bank account in Cuba and began making plans for a possible escape to that country.

The New Orleans exiles observed these events with

Juárez supported himself in New Orleans by rolling cigars and selling them in saloons. The spirit of many of his fellow exiles was broken by poverty and hardship, but Juárez remained optimistic, never losing sight of his revolutionary goals.

ILCE/CONSULATE GENERAL OF MEXICO IN NEW YORK

keen interest. As rebellion seemed close at hand in several states, Juárez and his friends decided that the time was now right for action from north of the border.

They threw their support behind the veteran revolutionary Juan Álvarez, a tough old guerrilla fighter whose mother had been an African slave. Álvarez had fought with both José María Morelos and Vicente Guerrero in the War for Independence, and he had a large, loyal following in the mountains south of the capital. At his side was Ignacio Comonfort, a Liberal Creole who had maintained close contact with the New Orleans group.

With the help and advice of Ocampo, Juárez, and their friends, the rebels in Mexico were finally able to declare their rebellion openly. They seized the port town of Acapulco, and there, on March 1, 1854, they "pronounced" their plan for a new government, drawn up in the small nearby village of Ayutla. The Plan of Ayutla, which some historians think was written by the New Orleans exiles and then diluted by the cautious Comonfort, was a modest document demanding little more than the end of the dictatorship and the establishment of a new constitution for Mexico.

Santa Anna's government remained unalarmed. For years, small rebellions had sputtered like damp firecrackers all over Mexico, and this one seemed no different than the others. Nevertheless, the aging president took to his saddle again and rode out to put the troublemakers in their place.

No very decisive battle followed, but Santa Anna returned to the capital claiming another grand victory and demanding a vote of confidence. He received one, but dissatisfaction with his regime continued to grow in the capital, and the money from the Gadsden Purchase was running out. Santa Anna stepped up the deposits to his bank account in Havana and, for safety's sake, sent his family to Cuba.

The tide was turning for the old politician. In June 1855 the rebels in Acapulco wrote asking the New Orleans exiles to join the revolution, which was gaining momentum all over the country. Ocampo

Mexicans, the moment of vengeance has come! The tyrant must fall!

—signs posted in
Mexico City, 1854

60

slipped across the border to fight in northern Mexico, while Juárez was selected to join the men fighting in the south. With the few dollars he was able to scrape together, Juárez left at the end of June for Acapulco, in the southern state of Guerrero.

Santa Anna had announced that political exiles could return to Mexico, but only after publicly swearing submission to his regime. To avoid the humiliating oath, Juárez decided to enter the country at the port of Acapulco, which was in rebel hands. This meant a long journey — by sea to Panama, by train across Panama (the Panama Canal had not yet been built), and then by sea again, up the Pacific coast to Acapulco. When he ran out of money, the ex-governor signed on as a sailor and loaded coal in exchange for his passage. He arrived in July 1855, penniless and ragged.

Juárez, by now almost 50 years old, did not make a very imposing appearance as he came to enlist in General Álvarez's army. Colonel Diego Álvarez, the general's son, looked at him doubtfully and asked what he wanted. Juárez answered simply that he had come to see how he could be useful in the fight for freedom.

"Can you write?" asked the colonel. Juárez said he could. The colonel outfitted the shabby volunteer with a fresh cotton shirt and trousers and took him to see the general. General Álvarez, who had never learned to write, asked Juárez to copy a letter, and was so pleased with the result that without further questions, he made the humble new recruit his secretary.

It was almost a week before anyone learned Juárez's identity, and even then, it was only by accident. A letter arrived from Ocampo addressed to Juárez with his title as a lawyer. The colonel suddenly made the connection. Juárez is a common name in Mexico, and no one had even suspected the true identity of the modest "secretary." Don Diego was, as he wrote later, "covered with embarrassment." When asked why he had not identified himself as the former governor of Oaxaca, Juárez replied: "What difference does it make?"

Juárez was immediately brought into the advisory

Send me Juárez, I pray you.
—IGNACIO COMONFORT
Liberal politician, later president of Mexico, from a letter written to Melchor Ocampo during the Revolution of Ayutla

council and listened to with respect. The focus was rapidly shifting from military to political matters as the revolutionary movement began to prevail, and the old soldier Álvarez was finding it increasingly difficult to keep up with events. The advice of his secretary, Benito Juárez, would grow more valuable to him every day.

On August 13, 1855, the Revolution of Ayutla came officially to an end when Santa Anna, realizing that his cause was lost, quietly departed for Cuba. The jubilant citizens of Mexico City made a gigantic bonfire of his gilded coaches in the middle of the town square.

It was now the rebels' task to form a constitutional government according to the Plan of Ayutla. *La Reforma* (the Reform), which was to alter the course of Mexican history, had begun.

> *It is just the sound of old cats, squalling in a tree.*
> —an official in Santa Anna's government, on the Revolution of Ayutla

In October 1855, revolutionary leaders from all over Mexico met in the city of Cuernavaca, south of Mexico City. The majority agreed that the office of president of Mexico belonged by right to Juan Álvarez, the man who had led the revolution. Álvarez accepted the honor. For his cabinet, the old soldier selected only people whom he knew personally. He gave the most important post, minister of the interior, to Ocampo, and made Comonfort the minister of war. A new post, minister of development, was created for the brilliant intellectual Miguel Lerdo de Tejada. Benito Juárez, lawyer and champion of education, desired no position at all, but he finally agreed to become minister of justice and public instruction.

The new government turned to the formidable task of restoring order to the bankrupt and divided nation. The Conservatives still clamored for the reestablishment of a powerful army, and of the Church as a central authority. A newly emerged monarchist faction called for a royal ruler and refused to recognize the part-Negro Álvarez.

Even the Liberals themselves, in power at last, quarreled with one another. The *puros* (the pure, or extreme, progressives) supported Ocampo and called for immediate, drastic changes, while the *moderados* (moderates) wanted the gradual reforms

THE LIBRARY OF CONGRESS

Juárez's daughters (left to right), Manuela, Felicitas, and Margarita, with his wife, Margarita Maza y Parada de Juárez, in Mexico City in 1861. Although Juárez's turbulent career often kept him away from Margarita for months at a time, the two were devoted to each other.

espoused by Comonfort. Álvarez's government began crumbling almost at once.

Comonfort, a skilled politician who sincerely believed that Mexico was not ready for radical reform, soon outmaneuvered his idealistic opponent, and Ocampo, after only two weeks in office, resigned in disgust in October 1855. The minister of finance, a former newspaper editor named Guillermo Prieto, quickly followed his example.

Although Juárez could see that the government was becoming increasingly unstable, he remained in office, determined to push some legislation through while there was still time. If even one reform law could be passed before the government fell, he thought, he might yet strike a blow at the oppressive system he had fought against all his life.

> *The people and the government shall respect the rights of all. Respect for another's rights is peace.*
> —BENITO JUÁREZ

Playing various officials off against each other and winning the support he needed with diplomacy and not a little guile, Juárez persuaded the legislature, on November 23, 1855, to pass one of the most controversial laws in Mexico's history.

The famous Juárez Law (usually known by its Spanish name *Ley Juárez*), was to be the first and most significant piece of legislation in the Mexican Reform. Actually a presidential decree rather than a law, the Ley Juárez reorganized the judicial system, eliminating special courts for the clergy and the military. At last, 21 years after the Loxicha incident, all Mexicans were equal before the law.

The effect of the new legislation was sensational. As Juárez wrote later, "It was the spark that produced the blaze of the Reform that later consumed the worm-eaten edifice of abuses and conventions; it was, in fact, a challenge to a duel, flung at the privileged classes." The new law became, overnight, the reform government's most dramatic illustration of progress.

The rich and powerful fought the Ley Juárez with everything they had. Priests and soldiers united with the wealthy to defend their traditional rights, and rebellions occurred throughout the country. It was the last straw for Alvarez, who had long since grown tired of political intrigue and of the cruel, petty snubs he suffered due to his African ancestry.

BRADLEY SMITH

Santa Anna's wife, Dolores, shared his tastes for extravagant clothes and luxurious surroundings. "Never had
the republic been mired any deeper in the muck of ig-
norance, want, and vice," wrote one historian; "never
had the republic sported such gorgeous plumes."

The moderados, who wanted to bring down the government and replace it with a more conservative one, convinced him that the uprisings were his fault. Álvarez had devoted his life to bringing peace and unity to Mexico, and now he was being held responsible for its current strife. In December 1855 he turned the presidency over to Comonfort.

Comonfort, a moderate, wanted to reconcile the old elite with the newly empowered masses, but the Ley Juárez created an apparently unsolvable dilemma. On the one hand, Comonfort could not revoke the law, even after he became president, because it was too popular; on the other hand, he could not enforce it without provoking violence.

Juárez had become a popular hero, but he also had powerful enemies. A very private person who rarely displayed emotion, he remained aloof from

The "Plan of Ayutla," released on March 1, 1854, was a political manifesto written by Santa Anna's opponents. At first accepted by only a handful of revolutionaries, the plan quickly gained adherents; by the spring of 1855, many of the nation's governors and military men had declared in favor of it.

ILCE/CONSULATE GENERAL OF MEXICO IN NEW YORK

the storms raging around him. To some he seemed a savior, to others a devil. He saw himself as a man of principle with a steadfast commitment to justice.

Comonfort's main goal was the preservation of a united country. When he assembled a new cabinet, after Álvarez left him in charge of the government, he felt it would be better not to include the supreme puro Juárez. Trouble had broken out in Juárez's home state of Oaxaca, and Comonfort asked the former governor to resume his office there and restore order.

It was with mixed feelings that Juárez boarded the old black carriage that was to carry him back to Oaxaca. He knew that with the Ley Juárez he had only begun the task of bringing legal equality to the people of Mexico, but he was confident that in time, other reform laws would be passed, and that eventually the old structure of injustice would collapse.

Once again Juárez threw himself into the task of governing Oaxaca. In the next 18 months, he built 54 new schools and a teacher-training institute, introduced modern agricultural techniques to the farmers of Oaxaca, and established a newspaper that many observers considered the best in the nation. He built a hospital, improved the roads, enlarged the national guard, and added courses in military science to the curriculum of his beloved Institute of Sciences and Arts. Among the best and most loyal officers in the national guard was one of Juárez's law students, a young Mixtec Indian named Porfirio Díaz. Benito Juárez — and Mexico — would see a great deal more of Díaz in the years to come.

While Juárez was building a prosperous Oaxaca, the national government was surging forward with legislative reform. The Ley Juárez, for all the protest it had aroused, was by this time proving effective, not only as a sound piece of legislation in its own right, but as an incitement to further reform. In June 1856 Miguel Lerdo de Tejada, who had replaced Prieto as minister of finance, produced another, even more revolutionary law.

The *Ley Lerdo* forbade the Catholic church, or any other institution, to own property beyond what

> *At last I have achieved my ambition. I have kindled the spark that will ignite the fire of reform.*
> —BENITO JUÁREZ
> on the passage of the *Ley Juárez*

Juárez (foreground), who had become minister of justice and public instruction after Santa Anna's ouster, meets with cabinet colleagues in late 1855. On November 23, 1855, the new government passed the *Ley Juárez* (Juárez Law), which reorganized the judicial system and made all Mexicans legally equal.

was needed for its own immediate purposes. For the Church, this was a tremendous economic blow. As the proprietor of over one-half the land in the country, it was by far the richest institution in Mexico; its annual income far exceeded that of the national government. Now the Church had to sell all its commercial holdings, which included mines, plantations, banks, factories, and rental properties.

Unfortunately, because peasants could not afford to pay the prices, most of the Church lands were sold to speculators and wealthy businessmen. The new owners exploited the workers and offered none of the social services that the Church had provided.

A third reform law, the *Ley Iglesias* (named for Comonfort's minister of justice, José María Iglesias), limited the fees that could be charged by the

ILCE/CONSULATE GENERAL OF MEXICO IN NEW YORK

THE NEW YORK PUBLIC LIBRARY

In this 19th-century wood-cut, Juárez holds the *Leyes de Reforma* (reform laws) in one hand and, with the other, chases away cowering figures representing the clergy and the nation's wealthy landowners.

clergy for the performance of baptisms, marriages, and burials. The poor were now allowed to receive the sacraments free; others were to pay only a small amount. It is important to remember that the Reformers, or "anticlericals," considered themselves good Catholics. Their goal was simply to limit Church control over civil matters, not to challenge its religious status. The reform laws succeeded in stripping the Church of its legal privileges and much of its income.

In February 1857 the government unveiled the

Juárez, the central figure in this portrait of the framers of the 1857 Mexican Constitution, displays the new document while pointing accusingly at the miter (headdress) of a bishop. The constitution prohibited all institutions — including the Catholic church — from owning more property than they required for immediate purposes.

ILCE/CONSULATE GENERAL OF MEXICO IN NEW YORK

THE NEW YORK PUBLIC LIBRARY

Pope Pius IX was outraged by the anti-Church provisions of the new Mexican Constitution. Unshakably opposed to all reform that threatened the Church's privileges, Pius regularly denounced Mexico's Liberal politicians.

crowning document of the Reform: the new Mexican constitution. Modeled in part on the U.S. Constitution, it included a bill of rights that assured freedom of speech, press, assembly, and education. The Ley Juárez and the Ley Lerdo were confirmed, thus assuring the separation of church and state. Slavery and all titles of nobility were abolished, and voting rights extended to all adult males. The government issued a decree requiring all public officials to take an oath of allegiance to the constitution.

The Catholic church, which vehemently condemned the constitution, announced that any Catholic who swore to support it would be excommunicated (denied the rights of church membership). President Comonfort was turned away from the cathedral of Mexico City on Easter Day, and when Juárez was formally reelected governor of Oaxaca in 1857, the Church refused to let him take part in the traditional inauguration mass. Instead he was sworn in at city hall, a simplification the unpretentious Juárez actually preferred.

Refusing to permit the president or the governor to attend mass was not the only step the Church took to oppose the new liberal constitution. In league with the army, it stirred up rebellion in many parts of Mexico, including the capital. In spite of the widespread unrest, presidential elections, as called for in the new constitution, were held in the fall of 1857. Although he was extremely reluctant to return to national politics, Juárez consented to Comonfort's request that he run for the presidency of the national supreme court.

Comonfort was reelected president, and Juárez received the top judicial office, which included the duties of vice-president. At the age of 51, Juárez stood first in succession to the presidency of his country. Comonfort gave him the important office of minister of the interior as well.

Juárez knew the danger of his new post. When on October 27, 1857, he boarded a stagecoach for the trip to Mexico City, he left his wife and family at Etla, promising to send for them when the political situation grew more stable. He was never to see Oaxaca again.

> *I shall have to manage as best I can without the prayers of the Church.*
> —BENITO JUÁREZ
> after the Church refused to offer a mass celebrating his election as governor

5

A Government in Exile

The law has always been my sword and my shield.
—BENITO JUÁREZ

The new government in Mexico City, born in blood and pain, was not to survive long. The Mexican bishops' threat to excommunicate all supporters of the constitution presented a terrible dilemma for the civil servants and military personnel, who were forced to choose between supporting the new law of the land or giving up their jobs.

Despite the good intentions of its founders, the constitution split Mexico into two camps. The divisions between the Liberals on one side and the Church and the army on the other pointed straight toward a new civil war. In mid-December 1857, a powerful Conservative general, Félix Zuloaga, took control of the capital, dissolved congress, and demanded that Comonfort revoke the constitution and declare a dictatorship.

Zuloaga had widespread popular support; even Comonfort, a devout Catholic, was of mixed mind about the constitution's anti-Church provisions. At last, believing that the rebellion against the constitution was sure to succeed, Comonfort decided to compromise with Zuloaga in order to save his government. He called on Juárez to change his politics also. Juárez was unshakable: "Truly," he said to

ILCE/CONSULATE GENERAL OF MEXICO IN NEW YORK

Appointed president of Mexico in December 1855, Ignacio Comonfort was ousted by Conservative rebels two years later for refusing to repeal the *Ley Juárez*. Under the terms of the 1857 Mexican Constitution (which the Conservatives had illegally abolished), Juárez, as head of the supreme court, succeeded Comonfort as Mexico's president.

Pushing his friend Juárez aside, Finance Minister Guillermo Prieto steps between him and a mutinous band of would-be executioners on March 15, 1858. Prieto's brave act saved the day, allowing Juárez to continue his leadership of the anticonservative forces in the 1858–61 conflict known as the War of the Reform.

Mexican working people relax in a cantina, or tavern. The Mexican lower classes' support for Juárez proved invaluable to the constitutionalists during the War of the Reform.

THE BETTMANN ARCHIVE

Comonfort, "I wish you good luck on the road you are going to take, but I shall not go with you."

Alone and desperate, Comonfort submitted to the general. "I have just exchanged my titles as president for those of a miserable revolutionary," he groaned. "But what is done is done, and there is no remedy. I accept everything, and God will show me the way." When Juárez arrived at his office the next morning, he found Zuloaga's soldiers waiting for him. The entry in his diary for December 17, 1857, reads simply, "I was arrested in the Palace."

Juárez spent the next three and one-half weeks in prison. Most of the remaining cabinet members resigned, and Comonfort found himself without Liberal support. Zuloaga was now joined by another Conservative general, Miguel Miramón, who had long opposed the Ley Juárez, and together the two generals demanded its repeal by presidential decree. When Comonfort hesitated, the Conservatives ousted him and declared Zuloaga president. As his last official act, Comonfort secretly released Juárez. Comonfort and his family then left Mexico for exile in the United States.

Juárez's diary states only that "On January 11, I was set free," but the events were more dramatic. Knowing he was just one step ahead of Zuloaga's men, he and two of his friends slipped out of the capital at night, carrying with them a copy of the constitution. They covered the first 30 miles on foot, sleeping in the fields and foraging for food. A mail coach took them from Querétaro just as that town fell to Zuloaga's army. At San Juan del Río they were nearly captured, and, according to the account of an observer, "owed their salvation to Juárez's incredible coolness."

At last, after eight days as fugitives, they reached Guanajuato, the capital of Jalisco Province. On January 19, 1858, Juárez declared that the constitutional government had been reestablished. Mexico now had two presidents and two governments. The stage was set for the three years of upheaval known to history as the War of the Reform.

Although Zuloaga had declared himself president, Juárez, as head of the supreme court, was Co-

> *We raise our pontifical voice to condemn, reprove, and declare null and void everything that the civil authority has done in scorn of ecclesiastical authority.*
> —POPE PIUS IX
> statement against the
> Mexican constitution

THE NEW YORK PUBLIC LIBRARY PICTURE COLLECTION

One step ahead of the pursuing enemy, Juárez and his followers ford a swollen stream during the War of the Reform. Despite the many reverses suffered by the constitutionalist forces during the first year of the conflict, Juárez never lost his habitual poise and dignity.

monfort's true constitutional successor to the office. He was the president by law. The constitution on which his claim to the title rested, however, had been abolished.

With Zuloaga in control of the presidential palace in Mexico City, Juárez's voice of protest was barely audible from Guanajuato. The United States minister to Mexico, asserting that he would find supporting the fugitive Juárez government "neither dignified nor agreeable," gave his country's official recognition to Zuloaga. Newspapers viewed Juárez's claims to power as something of a joke.

On the other hand, 11 Liberal governors, including former president Álvarez, now governor of the state of Guerrero, supported "the constitutional president," as Juárez called himself, and several generals rallied to his side. Juárez quickly chose a cabinet, with his old friend Melchor Ocampo at its head, and appointed General Anastasio Parrodi, former governor of Jalisco, commander in chief of the army. Juárez was no longer merely the head of an opposition party engaged in a political conflict. He was the leader of a full-scale revolt. The War of the Reform had begun in earnest.

The Liberals were in a weak position. With very little money, even less military experience, and no diplomatic recognition from any foreign country, Juárez's government was initially forced to take a defensive position in the war.

Juárez and his followers retreated from Guanajuato and set up camp in Guadalajara. Confident and courageous, Juárez was also unrealistic. He was sure that the toppling of Zuloaga's illegal government could be accomplished with a few quick military engagements. When he received the news that General Parrodi had been defeated in his first battle, Juárez appeared untroubled. "Our cock has lost a feather," he replied imperturbably. Soon, however, his confidence would be shaken, and his hopes all but shattered.

The next day news arrived that General Manuel Doblado, who was in charge of another section of the Liberal army, had been so badly beaten on his way to attack Mexico City that he had deserted and

They have invoked the sacred name of our religion—and have sought to destroy at one blow the liberty that Mexicans have won at the cost of sacrifices of every kind.
—BENITO JUÁREZ
on Zuloaga's government,
January 1858

taken his troops with him. Next, Juárez was informed that Colonel Antonio Landa, who had been in command of the Liberal regiment guarding Guadalajara, had rebelled and was marching his troops toward Liberal headquarters. Before Juárez and his cabinet had time to organize their defenses, they were seized by armed mutineers and herded into a small room in the Guadalajara statehouse.

Juárez's friend, minister of finance Guillermo Prieto, recorded the scene vividly some years later: "We were told that we were to be shot in an hour. . . . Some, like Ocampo, were writing their wills. Señor Juárez was walking up and down with incredible calm. . . . A tremendous voice cried, 'They are coming to kill us.' The soldiers entered the hall. . . . The terrible column halted, with loaded guns, opposite the door, and we distinctly heard 'Present arms! Ready! Aim!'. . . . Señor Juárez grasped the latch of the door, flung back his head, and waited."

At this point Prieto jumped in front of the president and cried out "Down with those guns! Brave men are not murderers!" The effect was electric. As Prieto "talked and talked and talked," the soldiers hesitated, finally dropped their weapons, and wept openly. Juárez's diary entry describing the event was typically understated: "On the 13th the Palace guard mutinied and I was taken prisoner by order of Landa, who led the mutiny. On the 15th I recovered my liberty."

Juárez was free, but he was no more secure than before. After issuing a moving statement to the nation, assuring the people that he and his followers would never surrender, he prepared to move his opposition government to yet another location. Pooling their small funds for food on the road, Juárez and his small band slipped away on horseback.

The first day out of Guadalajara, they were again attacked by Landa. Juárez knew his 100-man military escort could not hold off the enemy for long, and he told his cabinet members they must make a break for it after dark. Juárez, like a captain going down with his sinking ship, would stay to face the enemy. His ministers, however, unanimously refused to desert him. At last they all rode off together

A little Indian by the name of Juárez, who calls himself president of Mexico, has arrived in this city.
—Guanajuato newspaper article, January 1858

into the darkness.

The constitutional president and his nomadic government next made their way to the small town of Colima. There they learned that Parrodi and the remnant of his army had returned to Guadalajara only to meet with another decisive defeat. Juárez's army now only totaled about 350 soldiers. The president appointed Santos Degollado, a gentle, scholarly former college president, as head of what was left of his military forces. Deciding that Colima could not be defended, the liberal government once more took to the road.

After a long and exhausting journey, Juárez and his men arrived in the port city of Veracruz, which had remained loyal to Juárez. Here, after making a heroic, 300-mile trip with her eight children, Margarita was finally reunited with her husband. The Juárezes' oldest child was 14, the youngest an infant, but the almost penniless family walked most of the way from Oaxaca to Veracruz across trackless mountains, carrying their food and clothing on the backs of two burros. Veracruz, if unhealthy and uncomfortable, was at least safe. It was easy to defend, both by land and by sea, and its customs office provided the Juárez government with its main source of revenue.

The Liberals were always short of cash. Zuloaga's army, which was far larger, better trained, and better equipped, had the plentiful resources of the Catholic church to support it, while the army of Juárez's "constitutional" government was forced to depend on the thin trickle of funds coming through the port and on what money General Degollado could raise personally. As a fund-raiser, the commander in chief was a great asset to his government. He had been a professor of law, and his persuasive personality drew important contributions from Liberal sympathizers.

The Liberal army was essentially an amateur one, but the Conservatives were true professionals. Zuloaga's forces were led by three skilled generals, known as the "three M's." Miguel Miramón, a handsome, dashing young Creole of French descent, was the aristocrat of the group. Tomás Mejía, a full-

THE NEW YORK PUBLIC LIBRARY

During the War of the Reform, Tomás Mejía proved himself one of the Conservatives' most brilliant generals. Uneducated but deeply religious, he sincerely believed that by fighting Juárez and the constitutionalists, he was defending the Church.

blooded Indian, was a devout Catholic who fought for the Church with selfless passion. The third, called by one historian a "ruthless gangster-in-uniform," was Leonardo Márquez, the oldest and most savage of the three. When Márquez defeated Degollado at Tacubaya, he ordered the executions of not only all the prisoners but of the wounded in the hospital, plus the doctors and nurses. When a horrified country bestowed on him the nickname "Tiger of Tacubaya," Márquez accepted it as a compliment.

In an attempt to limit the amount of assistance the Church could offer the Conservatives, Ocampo and Juárez published ever more radical reform laws. According to their new legislation, all Church property was confiscated, every male religious order dissolved, many religious holidays eliminated, and freedom of worship established.

Degollado's few ill-trained troops would have had little chance against the "three M's" if the Conservatives had not had troubles of their own. In the autumn of 1859, dissension in the government enabled Miramón to seize the presidency from Zuloaga. Repeated outbreaks of yellow fever hampered the Conservatives' efforts to take Veracruz, set in the steamy marshland that breeds disease-bearing mosquitoes.

Moreover, popular sympathy for Juárez was growing. Day by day new recruits replaced those who fell, and independent guerrilla bands began to spring up throughout the country. Porfirio Díaz organized his own militia and led it in a string of impressive victories. In the north, Jesús Gonzáles Ortega built another formidable army; Ortega eventually replaced Degollado as commander in chief.

Despite their chronic shortages of money and equipment, the Liberal army fought on. For nearly three years the war continued, with neither side able to defeat the other decisively. The nation grew more and more anxious to see an end to the strife. Atrocities were committed by both sides; Conservatives shot prisoners of war; Liberals confiscated Church property and killed priests who refused the sacrament to their soldiers.

Although the Conservatives could field a larger

THE NEW YORK PUBLIC LIBRARY

Mexican soldier and politician Miguel Miramón, an ardent royalist, was appointed commander of the Conservative forces in 1859. Following the constitutionalist victory in 1860, he persuaded Napoleon III, emperor of France, to send a military expedition to Mexico to topple the Juárez government.

and better-equipped army, they lacked the broad popular support of Juárez's government. By 1860 the Liberal troops had become seasoned by experience, and the tide began to turn in their favor.

Guadalajara fell to the Liberal army in late October, and on Christmas Day 1860, General Ortega led the first section of his army into Mexico City.

THE BETTMANN ARCHIVE

The War of the Reform was over. The vanquished Miramón fled to France, leaving Mejía, Márquez, and Zuloaga to take refuge in the mountains.

On January 1, 1861, to the cheers of the public, General Ortega marched at the head of 25,000 troops into Mexico City. Seeing Degollado in the crowd, he stopped the parade, threw his arms

U.S. President Abraham Lincoln — shown with members of his cabinet in 1863 — was deeply sympathetic to Juárez's liberal, constitutional government. When Britain, Spain, and France (Mexico's three chief creditor nations) asked for U.S. participation in their armed intervention against the Juárez government, Lincoln flatly refused.

around the former general, and handed him a Mexican flag. Together the two patriots marched to the presidential palace in front of the victorious army. Ten days later, Juárez rode into the capital in his dusty old black carriage and, without fanfare, once again took up his office.

Although Juárez was the constitutional successor to Comonfort, he had never actually been elected president. His first official act was to call for a general election in order to establish a legal basis for his authority. Juárez's principal opponent was his own general, Jesús Gonzáles Ortega. A third candidate was Miguel Lerdo de Tejada, the author of the second great Reform law. On June 11, 1861, Juárez was overwhelmingly returned to office by popular vote.

Postwar Mexico was in a desperate situation; crime was rampant, unemployment severe, the national treasury empty. Miramón, the Conservative president, had borrowed large sums of money from European countries at unusually high rates; the government now owed more than $80 million to foreign powers and individuals.

Lack of money was not the only problem facing the new government. Mejía and Márquez, now hiding in the north and west, had formed dangerous guerrilla bands. Juárez, reluctant to impose order by force for fear of seeming dictatorial, was considered overly lenient by other Liberals. His policy of granting amnesty to Conservative prisoners involved him in endless disagreements with his own ministers, many of whom resigned in disgust.

Juárez had never been so much alone as he was during that first year back in the capital. Miguel Lerdo, his main economic adviser, had died suddenly, and other government aides on whom he had depended deserted him under the pressure of national recovery. On May 30, the president and the nation suffered an enormous loss. The outlaw forces of Márquez assassinated Melchor Ocampo; as a gesture of contempt for the government, Márquez ordered the statesman's body hung from a tree.

Juárez was deeply shocked by the brutal murder of his old friend, and the nation was outraged. San-

French Emperor Napoleon III joined Britain and Spain in their 1861 invasion of Mexico, aimed at collecting their debts. In 1862 the British and Spanish agreed to withdraw their troops and negotiate the debts, but Napoleon refused; France, he said, was now a permanent presence in the New World.

THE NEW YORK PUBLIC LIBRARY

tos Degollado mobilized a force to avenge the murder of the beloved Ocampo, but he was ambushed and killed almost at once. While the country was recovering from the news of this tragedy, a third general, the popular Leandro Valle, led a column of soldiers into the mountains to bring Márquez to justice. Valle, too, was captured and put to death. At last Porfirio Díaz forced Márquez to withdraw, but even he could not capture the Tiger.

The violence wracking Mexico from within was matched by the furious pressure from without. Hounded by demands for money from Spain, England, and France, Juárez was at last forced to suspend payments on the national debt for two years. The creditor nations immediately broke off diplomatic relations and dispatched warships to Veracruz. The Europeans' announced purpose was the retrieval of debts owed to their governments or subjects, but one nation had more sinister motives.

In desperation, Juárez turned to the United States for help. Unfortunately, the American Civil War had begun the very week that Juárez suspended payment of his country's debts. Abraham Lincoln, the first U.S. president in Juárez's time who considered Mexico "a friendly and sister republic," could offer his country's troubled southern neighbor nothing but sympathy.

Helpless, Juárez watched Spain land 6,000 troops at Veracruz in November 1861. By the beginning of 1862 the French and the English had followed suit. The three European powers invited the United States to join them in what was called "the Intervention," but President Lincoln emphatically declined the offer.

Mexico negotiated with the Europeans. At last, the representatives of Queen Isabella II of Spain and Queen Victoria of England agreed to relax their demands and allow Mexico to resume payment of its debt when it could, although at punishingly high rates of interest. Napoleon III of France, however, had no intention of losing a chance to extend his domain. He had always dreamed of building an empire like that of his famous uncle, Napoleon I. The French flag, he said, had come to Mexico to stay.

> *I am president by law. No republic is deserving of that name if it is not ruled by law.*
> —BENITO JUÁREZ

Even in a war studded with acts of barbarism by both sides, the savagery of Leonardo Márquez was awesome. He became known as the "Tiger of Tacubaya" after ordering the murder of wounded soldiers, civilian medical personnel, and even children, following a Conservative victory at Tacubaya in April 1859.

THE NEW YORK PUBLIC LIBRARY

6
Last Battles

Juárez had faced Santa Anna and outlasted him. He had survived the Zuloaga and Miramón regimes, and had defied the regular army and the Catholic church. Now he was confronted by a rich, powerful European nation that was determined to seize Mexico. It was the greatest challenge he had yet encountered.

Charles-Louis Napoleon Bonaparte had been elected president of France in 1848; four years later he proclaimed himself Emperor Napoleon III. Anxious to live up to his new title, Louis Napoleon sought fame and popularity through bold foreign adventures. Juárez's suspension of payments was the perfect chance for Napoleon to realize his dream of expanding French influence in Latin America. Embroiled in a civil war, the United States was not in a position to enforce the Monroe Doctrine against foreign intrusion. Furthermore, conservative Mexicans, as well as the Catholic church, would welcome a monarchy in their country. To the emperor, Mexico was ripe for conquest.

Napoleon III intended to create a French protectorate in the New World to serve as a base for the further expansion of his power. On April 27, 1862,

> *Whether or not we lose battles, whether we perish by the light of combat or in the darkness of crime, the sacred cause we defend is invincible.*
> —BENITO JUÁREZ

THE BETTMANN ARCHIVE

A protegé and supporter of Juárez, Porfirio Díaz fought with distinction in the War of the Reform and the French Intervention. Soon after the defeat of the French in 1867, however, he broke with Juárez, seeking power for himself. He ruled as a dictator from 1876 to 1911.

French and Mexican soldiers fight in the streets of Puebla on May 5, 1862. Although outnumbered and badly underequipped, the Mexicans — who were led by one of Juárez's most brilliant military commanders, Brigadier General Porfirio Díaz — inflicted a crushing defeat on the French.

BRADLEY SMITH

Maximilian's wife Charlotte — known in Mexico as *Emperatriz Carlota* — was overjoyed when her husband accepted Napoleon III's invitation to rule Mexico. An enthusiastic royalist, she particularly liked the idea of establishing an imperial dynasty in a country that had formerly been a republic.

THE BETTMANN ARCHIVE

6,000 French soldiers began a march from Veracruz toward Mexico City, the nation's capital. "We must now prove to France and to the entire world," announced the unshaken Juárez, "that we are worthy to be free."

And so they did. On May 5, when the powerful French force reached the city of Puebla, halfway between Veracruz and Mexico City, it met a smaller Mexican army of about 4,800 men. Although outnumbered and badly underequipped, the Mexicans defended Puebla valiantly and skillfully. Now a brigadier general, Porfirio Díaz led his forces to a resounding victory over the great army of France. Ever since then, Mexicans have celebrated the *cinco de Mayo* (fifth of May) in honor of that battle.

Proud as he was of his army's victory, however, Juárez knew that a long, hard battle lay ahead. A year later, with an additional 30,000 soldiers, the French again advanced towards Mexico's capital, planning first to conquer Puebla. A two-month siege finally forced the city to surrender, but only after its citizens had resorted to eating their cats, dogs, and even the leaves of orange trees. The road to Mexico City was now open.

THE BETTMANN ARCHIVE

Archduke Maximilian of Austria became emperor of Mexico in 1864 at the invitation of the Mexican Assembly of Notables. Although the "notables" were merely puppets who reflected the wishes of Napoleon III, Maximilian believed the Mexican people genuinely wanted him as their ruler. He was badly mistaken.

Juárez had planned to defend the capital, but he soon realized the hopelessness of his situation and moved north with his cabinet and what was left of the army. "Adversity dismays only contemptible peoples," he reminded his government, "our people

Maximilian and Charlotte arrive in Mexico on May 28, 1864. The new emperor sympathized with many of the reforms that had been instituted in Mexico, and even offered Juárez a position in the imperial government. Nevertheless, the only Mexicans who supported him were the Conservatives who had put him on the throne.

AUSTRIAN ALPENLAND NATIONAL MUSEUM

are ennobled by great deeds."

Upon entering Mexico City, the triumphant French set up a provisional government with two Conservative generals and a clergyman as its leaders. An "Assembly of Notables," made up of 215 Mex-

ITINERARIO DE LA RESISTENCIA
DEL PRESIDENTE BENITO JUAREZ (1863–1867)

ILCE/CONSULATE GENERAL OF MEXICO IN NEW YORK

Between 1863 and 1867, Juárez and his administration moved so frequently that the president's carriage became known as the "government on wheels." Juárez directed much of the war against Maximilian and the French from El Paso del Norte, which is now called Ciudad Juárez.

ican citizens, was chosen to help determine the country's future government.

Napoleon III had long desired to establish a Catholic imperial house in Mexico. Conservatives, rich landowners, and churchmen exiled from Mexico had assured the French that the people really wanted the rule of a European royal house. No one was surprised, therefore, when the puppet assembly declared that the country was now to be a hereditary monarchy with a Catholic prince as emperor. Napoleon III decided to offer the new Mexican throne to Archduke Maximilian, the younger brother of Emperor Franz Joseph of Austria.

The young, dashing, and handsome Maximilian seemed to be the ideal choice to serve as Napoleon's imperial pawn. He was good-hearted, well-bred, and, from all evidence, would be easily manipulated. Charlotte, his vain, ambitious wife, would undoubtedly be thrilled at the opportunity to establish a dynasty.

The Mexican royalists had no trouble arranging an "election" and producing a warm, personal invitation from the Mexican people. The young archduke, his head filled with romantic visions of a civilizing mission to a primitive continent, did not look into the invitation very closely. "Mexicans!" he responded, "You have asked for me! Your noble nation, by a spontaneous majority, has designated me to watch over your destinies!"

Undaunted by warnings from Mexican patriots and from their own European friends, Maximilian and Charlotte accepted the Mexican crown, went on to Rome for the pope's blessing (and instructions), packed their tapestries, and set sail. They saw themselves as leading a *mission civilisatrice* to bring light to the half-savage Mexicans. On the voyage over, Maximilian devoted his time to writing a handbook on court etiquette. The royal couple arrived in Veracruz on May 28, 1864.

Historians generally agree that Maximilian meant well. He seemed truly interested in developing the country and in gaining the support of the Mexican people. This heir to a thousand years of royal blood was, like a true aristocrat, above snobbery. He found Napoleon III "vulgar," but he sincerely admired Juárez. In an effort to be conciliatory, he freed many political prisoners and offered Juárez a job in his imperial government.

Juárez's answer is famous. "It is impossible," he replied in part, "for me to accept your summons; my occupations do not allow it. . . . It is true, sir, that history records the names of great traitors who have broken their oaths . . . and failed their own party and all that is sacred to a man of honor . . . but the present incumbent of the presidency of the republic who has sprung from the obscure mass of people will not succumb. It is given to men, sir, to attack the rights of others, to take their property, to attempt to take the lives of those who defend their liberty . . . but there is one thing that is beyond perversity, and that is the tremendous verdict of history. History will judge us."

Maximilian and Charlotte tried hard to make

> Great has been the reverse that we have suffered, but greater are our constancy and resolution, and we shall fight on with the greater ardor and with the certainty that victory will be ours because the nation still has life and strong sons to defend her.
> — BENITO JUÁREZ

themselves likeable and useful to their subjects. They spoke Spanish frequently, traveled throughout the land, served Mexican foods, and adopted Agustín de Iturbide, a grandson of Mexico's first emperor. Despite their efforts, however, their presence in Mexico was bitterly resented by all but a handful of Mexican royalists.

Furthermore, Maximilian was on the horns of a dilemma for which Napoleon III had not prepared him. Pope Pius IX had instructed the Catholic monarch in no uncertain terms to restore all the Church's property and privilege in Mexico. The good-natured emperor, however, found this task impossible. He could not turn back the hands of the clock, and in fact personally sympathized with many of the political, religious, and social reforms that had taken place in Mexico. His attitude alienated the Conservatives who had put him on the throne without winning over any of the Liberals.

Meanwhile, Juárez and the remnant of his government were in desperate straits. They were contending with the regular Conservative army as well as with the formidable French army. The great Liberal victory at Puebla was now a thing of the past. The French had won back every inch they had lost and now pushed steadily, implacably, northward.

Juárez could never rest or establish a secure seat of government. He and his three remaining ministers hid the state papers in a cave and hurried on from San Luis Potosí to Saltillo to Monterrey, always only one step ahead of the French. From Monterrey Juárez sadly sent his family to the United States for safety.

When Monterrey itself was threatened, Juárez climbed into his now famous old black carriage — "the government on wheels," as it was popularly known — and headed north. As bullets sprayed around the carriage, someone cried out to the coachman to gallop. "At a trot," Juárez corrected. "The president of the republic does not run."

At last Juárez and his ministers stopped in El Paso del Norte (now Ciudad Juárez), on the northern border of the country, and settled in for the duration of the war. From this distant post they

> *The Mexicans have a desperate and innate antipathy for kings. Anyone aspiring to the throne of Mexico ought to be extraordinarily happy if he escapes with his life.*
> —RICHARD HILDRETH
> American consul at Trieste, warning Maximilian not to become emperor of Mexico

watched as, one by one, the staunch patriots of the Liberal cause fell. Comonfort, the former president, had returned from exile in 1863 and now pleaded for a chance to redeem himself with an army command. His request was granted, but he was killed in battle almost at once.

Porfirio Díaz, "our Porfirio," as Juárez called him, was forced to surrender in Oaxaca and taken prisoner by the French, although he soon escaped and returned to the fight. Hardest for Juárez to bear, however, was the defection of his own men. Ortega asked him to resign, General Vidaurri went over to the Conservative side, and Juárez's personal attendants began to cross the border to safety in the United States.

Juárez was undaunted. He stubbornly clung to his cause and to his country. Asked if he could not better maintain his government in exile from the United States, he replied, "Show me the highest, most inaccessible, and driest mountain and I will go to the top of it and die there of hunger and thirst, wrapped in the flag of the Republic, but without leaving the national territory. That, never!"

There are circumstances in life in which it is necessary to risk everything if one wishes to go on living physically and morally.
—BENITO JUÁREZ

The United States invited Juárez to cross the border to safety, but he never even considered it. "It would be easier for the earth to move from its axis than that man from the Republic," wrote a Mexican admirer in 1865. "He works for the Republic and he will die in the Republic. If only one corner of the country remains, there you will be sure to find the president."

The French commander in Mexico, Achille Bazaine, was encountering as many difficulties as Juárez. His men were struggling with an enemy they could not subdue. The Mexicans fought so relentlessly that many French soldiers lost heart and deserted. To end the Mexicans' harassment of his troops, Bazaine persuaded Maximilian to take stricter measures against the troops of Juárez.

On October 3, 1865, the emperor signed an order that became infamous as the "Black Flag Decree." It stated that anyone caught bearing arms against the empire would be put to death within 24 hours. No trial was needed and no appeal possible. The decree applied not only to prisoners captured on the battlefield, but to civilians merely suspected of Liberal sympathies. Signing the harsh decree was the worst of Maximilian's many mistakes. It intensified the hostility of his opponents, weakened the support of the throne by moderate Mexicans, and ultimately brought about the emperor's own death.

In April 1865 the empire and the French army protecting it received its first major blow. The American Civil War had ended in victory for the Union, and the new American administration of Andrew Johnson — as staunchly behind Juárez as Lincoln's had been — was in a position to offer some cautious help to Mexico. Discharged Union troops with no work at home began to pour into Mexico to join Juárez's army. Surplus armaments were left conveniently near the camps of Liberal soldiers, who took them across the border at night without trouble. Finally, watchful American troops were massed along the frontier under General Philip Sheridan.

Most effective of all, however, was the diplomatic pressure the United States began to put on the French. Envoys reminded Napoleon III that his troops in Mexico were most unwelcome to a nation pledged to preventing European involvement in the New World. The message from Washington was clear: the United States wanted the French out of Mexico.

Mexico's relations with the United States, naturally very important to Juárez, were complicated by his own political situation. His chief justice and constitutional successor was General Ortega, who had opposed him in his last election and was now growing impatient for another chance at the office. Ortega was a good soldier but his ambitions made his loyalty questionable. He was suspected of trying to bargain separately with the French, and in 1864 he went to the United States on a private diplomatic mission. Reports came back to Juárez of anti-*Juarista* maneuvering and propaganda in the United States, where Ortega had settled down for a long stay. Ortega, said Juárez, appeared to belong "to the school of Don Antonio López de Santa Anna."

On December 1, 1865, Juárez's term was due to

To pity the wolf is to commit a crime against the lamb.
—GEORGES CLEMENCEAU
journalist, later French premier,
on the sympathy extended
to Emperor Maximilian

expire. Since it was impossible to hold an election with France currently occupying much of Mexico, the office of president should, according to the constitution, have gone to Ortega. Juárez believed that this was not in the best interests of the country. Although reluctant to act against the principles of the constitution, he felt that, in order to protect the cause for which he had fought so long, he had no choice but to extend his term by edict.

Using the special powers given to him by congress in 1861, he extended the terms of president and president of the supreme court until the end of the war. Strong protests followed. Some newspapers called Juárez a dictator, and he lost the support of his old friend Guillermo Prieto, the man who had saved his life in Guadalajara. The general public, however, continued to trust and respect Juárez.

That same year, 1865, Juárez's 15-month-old son, Antonio, died in the United States. His second son, Pepe, had died several months earlier. Margarita, who had borne so much, finally reached the

Mexican troops charge a French stronghold at Las Cruces during the French Intervention. In the early stages of the war, the constitutionalists were in such desperate straits that the U.S. government invited Juárez to take refuge in the United States. The Mexican leader refused even to consider such a move.

THE NEW YORK PUBLIC LIBRARY

limits of her strength. "The loss of my sons is killing me," she wrote her husband from New York City. "From the moment I waken I think of them. . . . I find no remedy, and the only thing that calms me is the thought that I shall die. My present life without you and without my sons is insupportable."

Juárez's personal and political burdens were heavy, but his military situation was beginning to improve. Napoleon III was feeling the increased pressure from the United States, and France was also

ART RESOURCE/SOTHEBY PARKE-BERNET

beginning to have problems with some of its closer neighbors. With Prussia, under Otto von Bismarck, the "Iron Chancellor," threatening its borders, Napoleon realized he would soon need all his military strength at home. His investment of money, men, and arms in Mexico had proved unrewarding. It was becoming increasingly clear that his plan for establishing an empire in the New World would have to be abandoned.

Maximilian was still living in a dream, literally

Mexican infantrymen fight off a French cavalry attack during the French Intervention. The morale of the Mexican constitutionalists received a tremendous boost early in 1866, when Napoleon III, convinced that war between Prussia and France was inevitable, ordered the withdrawal of all French forces in Mexico by the end of 1867.

devoting much of his time to collecting butterflies. He was profoundly shocked by a letter he received in early 1866. It was from Napoleon III, and it informed Maximilian that he could no longer look to France for support. Bazaine was to begin withdrawing his troops the next year.

Maximilian was too proud, or perhaps too naive, to abandon his throne. At any rate, Charlotte would never have permitted it. "Abdication amounts to . . . writing oneself down as incompetent, and this is admissible only in old men and idiots," she raged. Maximilian, confident that he could somehow salvage his Mexican empire, urgently requested Napoleon III to reconsider his decision, but the French ruler, determined to cut his losses, refused.

In July 1866 Charlotte decided to beg the emperor in person not to abandon her husband. When her pleas for help were ignored in Paris, she traveled to Rome to ask the pope for assistance. He, too, turned his back upon her. Faced with the certainty that her mission had failed, Charlotte lost contact with reality. She insisted that Napoleon had tried to poison her and that she was served by murderers. When she refused to leave the Vatican, officials sent for her brother, who took her to Belgium. There she lived for another 60 years, hopelessly insane. In October, a grief-stricken Maximilian learned both of his wife's madness and of the final refusals of assistance from Napoleon and the pope.

By early February 1867 the Juarist forces had regained much of the country. The Conservative army still fought fiercely, but it was hampered by shortages of men and supplies. In January Juárez and his government were almost captured when Miramón staged a surprise attack on their temporary headquarters in Zacatecas, in central Mexico. The president, refusing to leave until the last of his soldiers had been safely evacuated, escaped the city just as the attackers entered it. "If we had delayed a quarter of an hour more in leaving the palace," he noted later, "we would have given a happy moment to Miramón."

One by one, the cities still loyal to Maximilian fell. Still Maximilian did not take advantage of his

Achille Bazaine, the French commander in Mexico. Concerned about the ferocious resistance his troops were encountering from the Juárez forces, Bazaine persuaded Maximilian to sign the "Black Flag Decree," which imposed the death penalty on anyone who opposed the Mexican Empire.

THE NEW YORK PUBLIC LIBRARY

THE BETTMANN ARCHIVE

In 1865 American General Philip Sheridan — shown here leading a cavalry charge during the Civil War — received orders to mass his troops on the Mexican border. The move was part of the U.S. government's campaign to pressure the French into withdrawing from Mexico.

chances to flee. He joined Miramón and Mejía at Querétaro, 120 miles north of Mexico City, while Márquez headed for the capital to recruit fresh troops. Once in Mexico City, however, Márquez traitorously assumed supreme power, instituting a reign of terror that left the city in chaos and Maximilian without the reinforcements he needed.

The emperor and his men resisted their atttackers for a month in Querétaro. Surrounded by 27,000 Juarist soldiers, the besieged city soon ran out of food and water. Juárez's general offered Maximilian safe passage if he surrendered, but the emperor would not desert his men. At last, on the night of May 14, 1867, the city fell. Maximilian (ill with dysentery), Mejía, and the badly wounded Miramón were all captured. Meanwhile, Márquez had been forced to flee Mexico City. Disguised as a mule-driver selling charcoal, the Tiger of Tacubaya escaped to Havana, where he set himself up as a pawnbroker.

A law passed by the Juárez government in 1862 mandated the death penalty for any foreigner who conspired against Mexican independence, and for any Mexicans who assisted him. Maximilian, Mejía, and Miramón were tried under this law and, despite their attorneys' pleas for clemency, condemned to death. The principal charge against Maximilian was his own "Black Flag Decree," under which many Mexicans had died.

The sentence provoked a storm of protest. Juárez was flooded with requests for mercy from all over the world. The United States government urged Juárez to commute the sentence, and both the emperor of Austria and the king of Prussia wrote to Juárez, pleading for Maximilian's life. French liberal poet and novelist Victor Hugo wrote, "Act, Juárez, so that civilization may make an immense stride. . . . Let the nation at the very moment when it has annihilated its vanquished assassin remember that he is a man and absolve him." Italian revolutionary hero Giuseppe Garibaldi, who had been one of Juárez's most passionate supporters in Europe, added his voice to the international outcry.

Juárez responded to the many requests that he pardon Maximilian by saying that he had considered the question carefully in terms of justice and of the country. To an aristocratic European woman who begged for Maximilian's life, Juárez said, "If all the kings and queens of Europe were at your side, I could not spare his life. It is not I who take it away; it is my people and the law." Maximilian, along with Mejía and Miramón, was executed on June 19, 1867. His last words were, "May my blood put an end to the misfortunes of my new country."

When Juárez returned to his office in the capital a month later, the citizens greeted him with a wild celebration. Cheering crowds packed the streets, bands played, and the air was filled with flowers, confetti, and the thunder of bells, rockets, and cannons. When he reached the national palace, Porfirio Díaz handed him a bright, newly made flag, and then snapped to attention as the president ran his country's banner to the top of the flagpole with a shout of "Viva Mexico!"

Juárez, now 61 years old, once again went to work to restore his country. The tasks ahead of him were monumental. Mexico was prostrate, its industries almost at a halt, its credit shattered.

> *Thanks chiefly to Juárez, who had drawn out the force of the Mexican people, Mexico was now for the first time an independent and democratic nation.*
> —CHARLES ALLEN SMART
> American historian

Juárez's first act was to call for an election to legitimize his claim to the presidency. He was re-elected by a landslide vote, but there were clouds on the political horizon. His opponent had been his own protegé, the popular general Porfirio Díaz, who had served with honor and loyalty and was now looking for a better reward than a retired soldier's pension.

Juárez's candidate for the presidency of the supreme court, Sebastián Lerdo, had received many fewer votes than his chief, but he was elected. Díaz, with only a fraction of the votes received by Juárez and Lerdo, retired to his farm in Oaxaca to brood and grow sugarcane.

Lerdo worked well with Juárez, as did the new treasury secretary, Matías Romero. Together the three men made good progress in balancing the budget as closely as the nearly impossible circumstances allowed. Work on the railway line from Veracruz to Mexico City, abandoned during the war, was begun again, and educational opportunities were greatly expanded. Mexico, a country with one of the lowest literacy rates in the world, began the painful process of overcoming cultural prejudices and inertia. In 1874, 350,000 of Mexico's 2 million school-age children were students; it was a low ratio, but more than twice as high as it had been 50 years earlier.

French troops prepare to leave Mexico in 1866. Although Maximilian and his Mexican supporters found their position becoming increasingly precarious as the French withdrawal proceeded, they continued to fight determinedly.

THE NEW YORK PUBLIC LIBRARY

Celebrated French poet and novelist Victor Hugo wrote to Juárez in June 1867, begging the Mexican president to commute Maximilian's death sentence. Juárez refused, asserting that the decision was out of his hands. "It is not I who take [Maximilian's life] away," he said. "It is my people and the law."

THE BETTMANN ARCHIVE

The four years of Juárez's term saw the country well on its way to stability and security. The public loved and trusted him. By 1871, however, Juárez was confronted with both personal sorrow and political difficulties.

In January his beloved Margarita died at the age of 44. Although circumstances had kept the couple apart for much of their married life, they had been extraordinarily close. Juárez had depended on his wife for counsel as well as affection, and her death weighed heavily on him. All Mexico mourned with its leader, but the wave of national sympathy did not stop Juárez's political rivals.

Sebastián Lerdo, after a minor dispute with Juárez over a local election in Mexico City, resigned from the government in January 1871. It soon became clear that he intended to run for president in that year's national elections. Meanwhile, Porfirio Díaz, Juárez's 1867 opponent, had reorganized his political followers. When Juárez decided to run for his fourth term he thus found himself confronting parties of *Porfiristas* and *Lerdistas*, both prepared for a fight. Díaz in particular gained wide support by appealing to such dissatisfied elements in Mexican society as unemployed war veterans, churchmen, and the provincial strongmen whose wings Juárez had clipped.

Juárez's critics pointed to the fact that he had recently suspended constitutional guarantees in an effort to impose order on the country. He was accused of dictatorship, even by some members of his own party. Suggestions were made that, although he had been a great hero in his day, he was getting too old for the presidency.

The election results were so close that no candidate could claim a majority of votes. The choice had to be made by Congress, which, in October, declared Juárez the winner. It should have been a happy event, a demonstration that the country was grateful to Juárez for a lifetime of work, but it was not.

Flanked by the bodies of Generals Miramón and Mejía, Maximilian dies before a firing squad on June 19, 1867. Many people believed that Juárez would spare Maximilian's life at the last minute, but the Mexican president was unshakably convinced that the death sentence was in the nation's best interests.

AUSTRIAN ALPENLAND NATIONAL MUSEUM

The decision was the trigger for a rebellion. Porfirio Díaz, Juárez's once loyal old friend and former student, attempted to seize the office of president by force. He failed, but 200 rebels, including Díaz's brother Félix, were killed during the suppression of the coup. It was a national tragedy that cast a grim shadow over the beginning of Juárez's last term.

In the spring of 1872, Juárez, now 66 years old and showing evidence of his years of tireless activity, suffered two minor heart attacks. Struck by violent chest pains while he was working in his office on July 18, he went home and sent for his doctor. Although the doctor diagnosed a massive heart attack and ordered Juárez to bed, the stubborn president insisted on receiving several political callers, listening to their questions, and offering the advice they requested.

During the afternoon he asked his doctor if he was dying. As gently as he could, the doctor said he was, but Juárez kept right on working. He finally lay back to rest, and now there would be no more work for the exhausted leader. Just before midnight his strong heart stopped beating; Benito Juárez was dead.

The residents of Mexico City were stunned when, at daybreak on July 19, the city's huge cannon began to fire. The booming salute was repeated every 15 minutes, signaling the death of the nation's chief of state.

The funeral ceremonies for Juárez were as simple and dignified as he had been himself. The coffin, decorated only with the initials B.J., was followed to its resting place by thousands of mourners. The crowds lining the streets as the procession passed were silent and respectful. With none of the pomp and ceremony usually associated with state funerals, Mexico bid its leader farewell. Juárez now belonged to history.

Lerdo, who succeeded Juárez by law, held the office conscientiously until the end of the term. He was reelected in 1876, but soon afterward deposed by Porfirio Díaz, who ruled as a dictator for the next third of a century. Díaz was overthrown by a revolution in 1911.

[Juárez] was clearly the symbol of Mexico both to his own people and to other peoples, who had gained a new respect for his nation.
—IVIE E. CADENHEAD, JR.
American historian

THE NEW YORK PUBLIC LIBRARY

Porfirio Díaz presents a Mexican flag to Juárez in Mexico City on July 15, 1867. Juárez's return to the nation's capital triggered a tremendous public celebration and heralded the start of a new era in Mexican history.

ILCE/CONSULATE GENERAL OF MEXICO IN NEW YORK

Sebastián Lerdo de Tejada, brother of the author of the *Ley Lerdo*, was a leading Liberal who had loyally supported Juárez throughout the period of the French Intervention. An astute and popular politician, Lerdo was narrowly defeated by Juárez in the 1871 Mexican presidential elections.

Benito Juárez was an extraordinary figure. Born into a country with an oppressively traditional class system, he transformed himself from an illiterate shepherd boy into the nation's most powerful magistrate. In an era hugely complicated by military dictators, civil wars, banditry, and foreign intervention, he distinguished himself as a civilian who unfailingly placed his country's welfare above his own. Unlike most Mexican leaders, he never wore a military uniform, placing his trust in the power of the law before the power of arms.

In the Mexico of his time, Juárez's political ideals were truly revolutionary. Against the entrenched power of wealthy landowners and the mighty Catholic church, he proposed a legal concept that shook the foundations of tradition — namely, that all men, regardless of their race or class, should be equal under the law.

Juárez spent his life preserving the constitution

against its enemies and protecting the hard-won rights of the population from the grasp of an elite few. Through his efforts, the groundwork for great social changes was laid and Mexico made free from foreign rule to pursue its own destiny.

The Zapotec president's strength of character and notable career gave many Mexicans an increased respect for their Indian ancestry. Juárez enabled his countrymen not only to look back without shame but to face the future with hope and strength. Mexico's development has been slow and difficult, but its citizens have never forgotten Juárez or ceased to find inspiration in his devotion to freedom and democracy.

Juárez's tomb in Mexico City. After a lifetime of service to his country, the Mexican statesman and champion of democracy died of a heart attack on July 18, 1872. He was 66 years old.

ILCE/CONSULATE GENERAL OF MEXICO IN NEW YORK

Further Reading

Baker, Nina Brown. *Juárez, Hero of Mexico.* New York: Vanguard Press, 1942.

Blancké, W. Wendell. *Juárez of Mexico.* New York: Praeger Publishers, 1971.

Calcott, William Hardy. *Liberalism in Mexico, 1857–1929.* Stanford, Ca.: Stanford University Press, 1931.

de Trevino, Elizabeth B. *Juárez, Man of Law.* New York: Farrar, Straus, and Giroux, 1974.

Hanna, Seymore J. and Katheryn A. Hanna. *Napoleon III and Mexico: American Triumph over Monarchy.* Chapel Hill, N.C.: University of North Carolina Press, 1971.

Johnson, William W. *Heroic Mexico: The Violent Emergence of a Modern Nation.* Garden City, N.Y.: Doubleday & Co., 1968.

Meyer, Michael C. *The Course of Mexican History.* Oxford: Oxford University Press, 1979.

Roeder, Ralph. *Juárez and His Mexico: A Biographical History.* 2 volumes. New York: Viking Press, 1947.

Scholes, Walter V. *Mexican Politics During the Juárez Regime, 1855–1872.* Columbus, Mo.: University of Missouri Press, 1969.

Smart, Charles Allen. *Viva Juárez!* Philadelphia: J. B. Lippincott Co., 1963.

Syme, Richard. *Juárez: The Founder of Modern Mexico.* New York: William Morrow & Co., 1972.

Young, Bob and Jan Young. *The Last Emperor: The Story of Mexico's Fight for Freedom.* New York: Julian Messner, 1969.

Chronology

March 21, 1806	Born Benito Pablo Juárez in San Paulo Guelatao, Oaxaca, Mexico
Dec. 17, 1818	Moves to the state capital, the city of Oaxaca
Sept. 28, 1821	Mexico wins its War for Independence against Spain
1821–27	Juárez enters seminary and studies for priesthood
1828	Begins study of law at the Oaxaca Institute of Sciences and Arts
1831	Receives law degree, elected to Oaxaca's city council
1833	Antonio López de Santa Anna takes over presidency of Mexico Juárez elected to the Oaxaca state legislature
1836	Santa Anna attacks Texan-American settlers at the Alamo
July 31, 1853	Juárez marries Margarita Maza
1846	Elected to the national Congress Mexican-American War breaks out over Texas boundary issue
1848	Juárez elected governor of Oaxaca Mexican-American War ends; U.S. annexes Mexican territory
1853	Juárez exiled by Santa Anna's Conservative government; goes to U.S. city of New Orleans
1855	Returns to Mexico to join rebellion against Santa Anna Named minister of justice and public instruction after Santa Anna's government falls *Ley Juárez*, a law reforming Mexico's judicial system, passed
1856	Juárez named governor of Oaxaca for second time
1857	Mexican constitution, restricting military and clerical privileges and assuring basic rights to all citizens, adopted Juárez elected president of the supreme court, automatically making him national vice-president
Dec. 1857	Félix Zuloaga seizes power, Juárez is briefly jailed
1858	Juárez declares himself president of constitutional government in opposition to Zuloaga's Conservative regime; War of the Reform begins
1861	Juárez is elected president after Conservative defeat; suspends payments of Mexico's foreign debts England, Spain, and France land troops in Mexico
May 5, 1862	French troops defeated by Mexicans at Puebla
1863	French occupy Mexico City Juárez proclaims resistance government
1864	Maximilian becomes emperor of Mexico
1867	France withdraws troops from Mexico; Juárez returns to Mexico City; Maximilian executed; Juárez reelected president
1871	Reelected president
July 18, 1872	Dies of a heart attack

Index

Dennis Wepman has a graduate degree in linguistics from Columbia University and has written widely on sociology, linguistics, popular culture, and American folklore. He now teaches English at Queens College of the City University of New York. He is the author of *Simón Bolívar, Jomo Kenyatta, Alexander the Great, Hernán Cortés,* and *Adolf Hitler* in the Chelsea House series WORLD LEADERS   PAST & PRESENT.

Arthur M. Schlesinger, jr., taught history at Harvard for many years and is currently Albert Schweitzer Professor of the Humanities at City University of New York. He is the author of numerous highly praised works in American history and has twice been awarded the Pulitzer Prize. He served in the White House as special assistant to Presidents Kennedy and Johnson.